RA Now

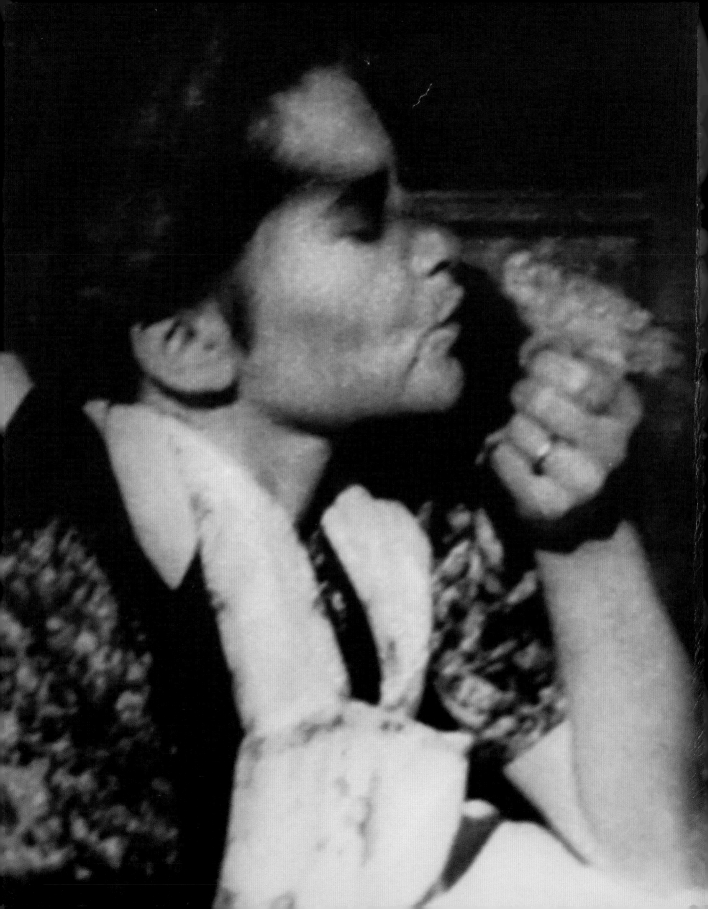

RA Now

Royal Academicians
from Anish Kapoor to Zaha Hadid

SUPPORTED BY

AUCTION PARTNER

Sotheby's

Royal
Academy
of Arts

Contents

As a long-term supporter of the Royal Academy of Arts, JTI is delighted to be involved in 'RA Now' featuring the work of the current Academicians. 'RA Now' provides an exceptional opportunity to celebrate a unique moment in the RA's history where the work of an immensely talented and diverse group of artists can be seen in one exhibition. It is especially poignant that today's Academicians will be helping to secure the RA's future for generations to come.

Martin Southgate
Managing Director, UK
JTI

It is sometimes overlooked that the Royal Academy was founded some 244 years ago on the principle of being an artist-run organisation that received no funding from the state. Through the support of loyal Friends, ticket sales and sponsorship, the RA has remained true to this principle and continued to thrive as a centrepiece of the nation's cultural life, exhibiting the greatest contemporary and historic art.

In this context, 'RA Now' is a significant undertaking to help ensure that the Academy can join its current premises to the galleries in Burlington Gardens, so expanding to create an ambitious new international centre for visual culture. Bringing together such an array of talent for this exhibition and auction is a testament to the skills of those most intimately involved, from Allen Jones RA, who co-ordinated the project, to RA Trustee Anya Hindmarch, who chaired the committee that included Richard Chang, Sir David Chipperfield RA, Michael Craig-Martin RA, Mollie Dent-Brocklehurst, Tracey Emin RA, Stephen Fry, Frank O Gehry Hon RA, Candida Gertler, Zaha Hadid RA, Jay Jopling, Anish Kapoor RA, Jeff Koons RA, Michael Landy RA, Natalie Massenet, Grayson Perry RA, Stefan Ratibor, Ed Ruscha Hon RA, Jenny Saville RA, Charlotte Stockdale, Sir David Tang, Gillian Wearing RA, Alannah Weston and Alasdhair Willis.

Primarily though, the success of 'RA Now' is thanks to the support of the Academicians and Honorary Academicians who donated works. There are well over 100 artists represented and, as this catalogue shows, these celebrated artists have donated significant works. It is the first time in the history of the Academy that such a number of Royal Academicians has exhibited under one roof and from my perspective, both personally and in my role as auctioneer and Deputy Chairman of Sotheby's, it is a tremendous honour to be involved in ensuring the future of such a wonderful institution.

Lord Poltimore
Deputy Chairman, Sotheby's Europe

Sotheby's

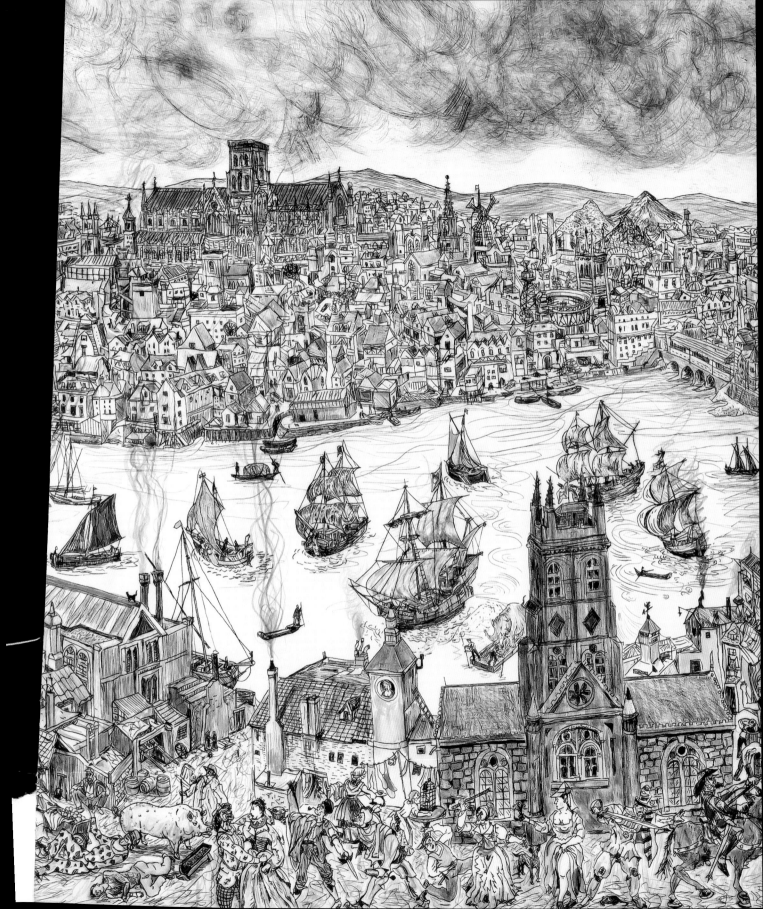

President's foreword

This is a very important moment for the Royal Academy. Featuring work entirely from my fellow Royal Academicians and Honorary Members, this exhibition and fundraising auction achieve two objectives: to show Academicians' support and personal contributions for the Burlington Project, and to display the work and achievement of the current membership.

The Academy is entering the most significant phase of its development since its move to Burlington House on Piccadilly in 1868, exactly 100 years since it was first established by George III. The purchase of 6 Burlington Gardens from the Government in 2001 – virtually doubling the site to 2.5 acres – set in train a long process of debate and discussion during which the Academy reformed its governance and reinvigorated its sense of itself and its potential. The building's mixed occupation over the intervening years has both helped us become familiar with this large and complex building, and to determine how best to develop its use into the future activity of the wider Academy.

One of the most essential and symbolic developments will be the establishment of a coherent link connecting Burlington House with 6 Burlington Gardens. This will allow future visitors to pass through the heart of the Academy, experiencing the atmosphere of the historic cast corridor and revealing one of our best kept secrets: the Royal Academy's Postgraduate Schools. It has been a longstanding ambition to give them the prominence they deserve.

The redevelopment of 6 Burlington Gardens will see the creation of a new double-height auditorium seating 300 people, enabling the expansion of our Academic Programme and offering new possibilities for debate and discussion. The refurbishment of three first-floor galleries will allow us to develop our exhibition programme far beyond our present capability (for Architecture in particular) and above all for our own Members and students. The new Learning Centre builds on our experience in art education by introducing a far wider range of visitors to one of the nation's great institutions. Many of the Academicians give time to teaching here so visitors will now have the chance to experience a living Academy, and the strengths and differences of an institution run by artists.

The Burlington Project also includes the major refurbishment of the Keeper's House in the southeast corner of Burlington House, substantially extending the space for the exclusive use and comfort of our Friends, and now including the small and previously inaccessible garden. Finally, the project will increase the circulation space and visitor amenities (tested to the limit during the David Hockney exhibition) in the entrance hall of Burlington House, with clearly lasting benefits for all.

Academicians have been closely involved in the detailed shaping of our future direction, and their present consensus around the master plan of Sir David Chipperfield RA is the culmination of that long debate. As can be seen from the numbers who have donated a work to this exhibition, our Members are now generously demonstrating their support of the Burlington Project and the rewards it will bring to the Academy, its supporters and visitors.

'RA Now' will secure vital funds to help us realise the Burlington Project, which is progressing well. This summer we received a stage one pass for a £12.7 million grant from the Heritage Lottery Fund. This initial support demonstrates the transformative potential of the Burlington Project. Support from the HLF will allow us to investigate further our plans for exploring, revealing and celebrating our heritage through our new learning programmes. In order to submit a stage two application to the HLF in the summer of 2013, we need to secure further matching funding of £12 million.

As well as being an important fundraising auction, the exhibition itself is a rare opportunity to celebrate the wide range of our current Membership. Within the categories of Painting, Printmaking, Sculpture and Architecture, the regular elections of new Members brings fresh energy, talent and views, all of which benefits the organisation as much as the experience and wisdom of our long-standing Members. In the last 10 years we have elected 39 Academicians. Of the total of 80 Members under the age of 75 this represents a renewal of 49%. As with all Academicians, these new Members represent all areas of artistic and architectural activity, with the common denominator that their professional achievement is esteemed by their peers. 'RA Now' is a demonstration of that range, and as such represents a broad view on the state of contemporary art and architecture.

It will be no surprise for you to learn that artists, no matter how much they feel the value of the cause, can be highly allergic to auctions. It is a moment when the iron imperatives of professional reputation can collide uncomfortably with private conscience. For the sake of prices, being dead is by far the better option, but one that artists aren't alone in finding unappealing. In view of that, I am immensely grateful to Allen Jones RA who has deployed his abundant experience and tact to nurture and steer 'RA Now'. On the metaphorical parade ground with his fellow members, Allen stepped forward to make those calls. We thank our Members and Honorary Members for donating such strong representative work.

We also owe a debt of gratitude to our exhibition supporters, JTI, longstanding patrons of the Academy, whose support for this ambitious exhibition is very much valued by the Academy and its Members. We also thank Sotheby's, and in particular Lord Poltimore for his guidance, and their generous support in funding the exhibition catalogue. We anticipate that it will remain of great interest for some considerable time as it records a particular moment in the Academy's long history whilst anticipating the promise of its future.

In the end, the Royal Academy is made from the vision of exceptionally creative personalities, and will therefore contain all the elements of character, wit, invention and imagination that you might expect. Yes, we are a great historic institution and our buildings and appearance are amongst the grandest – north and south, the porticoes are ranged with sculpted figures of achievement and authority – but putting our delight in art and colour, warmth of feeling and intuition at the heart of the nation's life, teaching, influencing debate and contributing a sense of aesthetic value where it can most help, this is our true but happy purpose. Because of what they see and feel, the visionary artist and architect is always ambitious for art. Their calling demands it. Given your help, we intend that to be reflected in this great project.

Christopher Le Brun
President

The Academy: to now; now; from now
Mel Gooding

There is and never has been an independent organisation of artists and architects anywhere in the world at any time that could possibly muster a body of work of this consistency of quality, breadth of vision and diversity of style and manner, and to do it with a view to the imaginative improvement of its own premises as a place of presentation, of critical discourse and of good feeling about the necessity to the health of our society of the visual arts and architecture. The Royal Academy itself has, of course, had other, earlier periods of superlative achievement. There was a time when Constable could remark the artistic ordnance of Turner on Varnishing Day[1]; two masters whose simultaneous membership in the Academy of its day – not to mention that of two great architects, Robert Smirke and John Soane – alone assured it an historical eminence. The first membership of the Academy in 1769 was itself of great distinction indeed, including, as it did, the painters Joshua Reynolds, Thomas Gainsborough, Benjamin West, Angelica Kauffmann and Richard Wilson, and the architect William Chambers, among its mere 34 Members.

But, astonishingly, there has never before been a comprehensive cross-section presentation of works by the Members of the Academy only. The annual Summer exhibitions – from the very first one in the year of its foundation – have always been generously and, by the founder's intention, open to submission from artists outside the Academy. This makes the present exhibition 'RA Now' momentous indeed. And it is in support of a development itself momentous for the London art scene now, and potentially for the future of British art and culture in every respect. For the extension of its premises into a brilliantly reconfigured suite of galleries and rooms in the magnificent palazzo of 6 Burlington Gardens will create new possibilities of exhibition and display, of scholarly and popular presentations, lectures and demonstrations that will enhance public knowledge and critical appreciation of the artistic and architectural events that make up the calendar of the Academy's year, and which in the last 40 years have succeeded in re-establishing the Academy as a forum central to our national culture. Such events, popular and specialist alike, feed naturally if imperceptibly into the general culture as they resonate in different ways and with different sonorities within the discourses of the visual arts. For the Academy has become in the last 40 years a powerhouse for the promotion and dissemination of world and British art and architecture and a generator of cultural energies in the land.

This is an extraordinary achievement, for in mid-twentieth century the Academy had deteriorated into a reactionary club-like establishment dominated by a faction determined to preserve what it ignorantly regarded as traditional values in Art, and which had set its face against any kind of modernism in painting and sculpture. So much so that the best British artists of the time, from Henry Moore and Barbara Hepworth to Victor Pasmore, William Scott, Ceri Richards and Patrick Heron, would not set foot, metaphorically speaking, inside the building in Piccadilly. Exceptions were of course made when the Academy put on one of the great, sometimes epochal, winter exhibitions that had been since the nineteenth century one of its principal financial mainstays, and which had maintained for it a vestigial degree of critical respect. Few were the serious younger modern artists of the time who did not attend – and find themselves deeply affected by – the stupendous Italian exhibition in 1930, the great catalogue of which remains a major historical and academic source in more ways than one. Ironically, many of the traditionalist academicians themselves were dismissive of the .... dominated the show. As Kenneth Clark recalled many

1 'Turner's ordnance': in 1832 Constable was putting finishing touches to his painting *Opening of Waterloo Bridge*, which was hung next to a sea-piece by Turner. After a while Turner, who had been looking first at Constable's and then at his own painting, fetched his palette and without a word 'placed a round daub of red lead, somewhat larger than a shilling, on his grey sea… The intensity of the red lead, made even more vivid by the coolness of his picture, caused even the vermilion and lake of Constable to look weak. I came into the room just as Turner left it. "He has been here", said Constable, "and fired a gun".' (*Autobiographical Recollections by the late Charles Robert Leslie*, edited by Tom Taylor [London, 1860])
2 Kenneth Clark is quoted in James Fenton, *School of Genius: A History of the Royal Academy of Arts* (Royal Academy, London, 2008).
3 For an account of the 1949 Annual Dinner see Fenton, op cit.
4 Thomas Monnington is quoted from an interview in *The Christian Science Monitor*, 29 May 1967. His British Council House ceiling was unveiled in 1956.

public took a fancy to that kind of painting their own degraded realism would be at a discount'.[2]

The disgrace of the PRA Sir Alfred Munnings's drunken rant at the newly revived Annual Dinner in 1949 was long remembered: in it he ridiculed modernism, and especially that of Picasso and Matisse, and claimed (falsely as it seems) that Winston Churchill (present at the dinner as an Honorary Academician Extraordinary) actively sympathised with him in his philistinism, not to mention the Archbishop of Canterbury and the Lord Mayor and City Aldermen, whose 'support' he seemed to think confirmed his case. Broadcast live to the nation on the BBC, it made a deep impression on many young and middle-generation artists (including those within the Academy whom Munnings thought were 'shilly-shallying' in that they actually felt that 'there [was] something in this so-called modern art'), and confirmed the deeply negative view of the Academy of those artists who might be described as '*refusés*' as well as those who were never invited to join.[3]

Times were to change drastically, but not immediately. The Royal Academy has long shed its reputation as an exclusive self-perpetuating club of mediocre gentlemen professionals (with ladies occasionally admitted) whose range of artistic ambitions was generally constrained by narrow definitions of stylistic propriety (naturalistic) and of permitted subjects (figurative, portraiture, landscape, still-life) within an over-arching panoply of strictures regarding the hierarchy of genres, and whose production of work was largely a matter of commission or of convention. Contemplating the marvellously diverse array of work presented here by the contemporary Academy it might be proper and salutary to acknowledge the contributions of certain key players in some of the crucial events in that progress towards the present unprecedented vitality of the Academy and the giddy prospect of a brilliant future at the heart of British artistic and architectural culture.

The first steps into the modern(ist) world were made possible by the election to PRA of Thomas Monnington in 1966. Monnington had been a quietly conventional landscape painter and a moderately successful figurative muralist who, in 1953, had responded to a commission for the ceiling of the new Council House of Bristol with geometric designs on a vaguely scientific theme (he executed the painting in situ in tempera, that most traditional of media, having fresh eggs for the emulsion delivered each day). Thereafter he devoted himself as an easel painter as well as a decorative muralist to a painstaking geometric abstraction, and was accordingly the first President committed in his own work to non-figuration. Monnington was not a distinguished painter, but he was thoughtful and tolerant in his approach to art: 'I happen to paint abstracts, but surely what matters is not whether a work is abstract or representative, but whether it has merit.'[4] He continues with a quiet dig at his academic colleagues: 'If those who visit exhibitions – and this applies to artists as well as to the public – would come without preconceptions, would apply to art the elementary standards they apply in other spheres, they might glimpse new horizons. They might ask themselves: Is this work distinguished or is it commonplace? Fresh and original or uninspired, derivative and dull? Is it modest or pretentious? ... You can apply the same judgments to it as you can to traditional works.' A similar critical open-mindedness regarding the present exhibition is unlikely to be encumbered by any 'preconceptions' regarding the 'abstract', the 'representative' or the 'traditional', but we should not underestimate just how bravely radical a position Monnington, as PRA, was taking at the time.

His direction of travel was clearly indicated by his welcome to the Academy, in 1968, of the exhaustive and hugely successful '50 Years Bauhaus' exhibition from Germany. Its impact on the public and artists alike was enormous. But that was an historical show, albeit one celebrating a great modernist manifestation. More significant within the Academy's own history, however, was Monnington's direct patronage of 'British Sculpture 1972', a gathering of 24 more or less abstract sculptors, curated by Bryan Kneale, who had accepted his election as an ARA on the understanding that he would be so commissioned. It was not that the abstract revolution in British sculpture of the 1960s had gone unheralded – Anthony Caro had enjoyed a hugely influential major show at the Whitechapel Gallery in 1963 and a retrospective at the Hayward in 1969; the defining 'New Generation: Sculpture' at the Whitechapel in 1965 had been followed there in 1966 by Kneale's own mid-career retrospective. What was significant was that the new abstract sculpture was here ensconced and celebrated within the very walls of Burlington House. The bastion stormed with help from within!

It was a remarkable moment. Apart from the annual mixed bag of the Summer shows, it was the first exhibition of contemporary art at the Academy. Its catalogue essay constituted a kind of manifesto, written by the generously visionary and subtly radical Bryan Robertson, until recently the Director of the Whitechapel Gallery, which through the fifties and sixties had in London's East End pioneered the presentation of post-war European and American modernism and of the very best contemporary British art.[5] Robertson's appearance in this context was rather like Henry Fonda turning up *as a villain* in *Once Upon a Time in the West*, only the other way round, so to speak. The guiding spirit of modernism in London, and critical friend to his younger contemporaries, in the catalogue he was diplomatically wary: 'It would seem sensible and agreeable for [RA Members] to allow aesthetic allegiances other than their own to be ventilated within its premises from time to time…' But he was unequivocal about the implications of Kneale's ground-breaking show: '… it will be an historic event in the annals of the Royal Academy, and could establish a positive and healthy precedent for the future relationship between the Academy and British art as a whole.'

A shining idea was in the air: that the Academy might once more play a vital and *vitalising* role in British visual culture, and extend its functions in actively promoting the best painting, sculpture and architecture of its time – national and international – through exhibitions and education. On New Year's Day 1977 it found trenchant expression in a *Spectator* article by Norman Rosenthal entitled 'The future of the RA': ' … the dominant economic problem of the RA is that as an exhibiting organisation it is grossly under-used and under-developed.' The beautiful top-lit galleries of Burlington House and its central metropolitan position, he argued, respectively gave it advantages over the Hayward and Tate; in this latter respect it was comparable to the Grand Palais in Paris, and it could come to fulfil a similar role in our own national culture. The 'Summer Exhibition' provided a market for artists, and 'a large, confused view of mostly traditional art activity that has taken place during the year'; Rosenthal was adamant, however, that it must be 'not only improved upon but supplemented by a carefully planned programme of contemporary art both from this country and from abroad. The increasing internationalism of the language of art, though it allows any number of local and personal differences, is something that is denied only at the risk of burying critical faculties in the sand.' Such a programme would slowly win back 'the support of many significant artists, who for their own legitimate reasons have turned their backs in this century on what was meant to be their own platform'.

Many of those artists had found their platform at the ICA, which had been founded in 1946 as a kind of alternative modern academy, with a programme of exhibitions and events promoting ideas and creativity in the arts and sciences. In his article Rosenthal, who until recently had been the ICA's

5 Bryan Robertson curated a succession of 'New Generation' exhibitions at the Whitechapel Gallery: 'Painting' (1964), 'Sculpture' (1965), 'Interim' (1966).

6 'The return of the exile': *The Exile's Return: Toward a Redefinition of Painting for the Post-Modern Era* by Thomas McEvilley was published in 1993 by Cambridge University Press.

controversial exhibitions officer, was scathingly dismissive: 'The [ICA] is now utterly defunct, and should be closed down once and for all.' (The Institute is, as it happens, still alive and kicking.) He continued: 'However startling the proposal, there is no reason why the RA should not take upon itself that programmatic role and become the major forum for new art again – as it was in its first hundred years.' It was a brilliant job application: the recently elected PRA, Sir Hugh Casson, a worldly progressive anxious to promote change and financial stability, had long had similar ideas, and circulated the article to the Members of the Academy Council. A few months later he created the post of Exhibitions Secretary for Rosenthal.

Under the direction of the incomparable Rosenthal, with the critical support of successive academician Exhibitions Committee chairmen, including Allen Jones and Tom Phillips, the exhibitions programme of the Academy more than fulfilled his thrilling prescription: through the 1980s and '90s it brought to the heart of London a series of magnificent national surveys of twentieth-century art: German (1985), British (1987), Italian (1989) and American (1993), each presenting work from the great modernisms, but bringing the picture of the art in those countries up to the living present. Partial, contentious and idiosyncratic as the selection of art and artists at times may have been (and a good thing too), they enabled a wide public and a generation of younger British artists to see clearly the characteristic national patterns, concentrations, surges and dislocations of artistic energy as they occurred through the twentieth century. They were visual and intellectual feasts, which could not but effect enhancements of knowledge and shifts in sensibility in those who attended them: to recall Monnington, 'those who came without preconceptions might glimpse new horizons'.

In 1981 Rosenthal, with Nicholas Serota and Christos Joachimides, co-curated 'The New Spirit in Painting', the hugely influential Academy show that was a defining event in the return of the 'exile' – expressive figurative painting – to the international scene.[6] Painting was back after a decade or more in which its validity and viability as an expression of the contemporary consciousness had been severely challenged by new media. The exhibitions from those years – and on to the present - indeed established the Academy as a major force within British visual culture: they perfectly complemented in-depth surveys of individual contemporary artists and experimental and more locally focused events at the Serpentine Gallery, Camden Arts Centre and, especially, the brilliantly international programme under the direction of Serota at the Whitechapel Gallery through the 1980s and continued there since.

With 'Sensation' in 1997 the Academy effected its most dramatic presentation of immediately contemporary work, showcasing controversial paintings and sculptures from a single collection. There is no need here to rehearse the arguments and events, internal antagonisms and public furore of the occasion; what was important, historically, was that the Academy had, for the first time, momentarily placed itself at the heart of the immediate action in the artistic hurly-burly of the day. A new generation of successful artists would take account of that when their opportunities for election came round. Several artists in that show are now Royal Academicians, represented in the present exhibition.

Without question the exhibition programme of the last 30 years has played a crucial role in the establishment of the Academy as a cultural force, including, as it has, stupendous exhibitions of classic art from the Renaissance to Post-Impressionism, modern art from Russian collections, a survey of late medieval English art, great retrospectives of modern American and European masters, and panoramic surveys of Japanese, Aztec, African and other world arts. Artists and student artists have been inspired, lives have been enriched, and the Academy has been able to raise crucial cash without resort to the public funding that Rosenthal had advocated (wrongly as it has turned out) in his *Spectator* article as a prerequisite for the future he envisaged. There have been spectacular recent successes in this respect: Anish Kapoor's amazing sculptural extravaganza in 2009; the moving and revealing 'The Real Van Gogh: the Artist and his Letters' in 2010; David Hockney's astounding 'The Bigger Picture' earlier this year.

The Summer show comes and goes, providing a platform for Academicians (and others) and attracting its annual thousands; the ingeniously and gracefully inserted Sackler Galleries, replacing the inadequate old Diploma Gallery, have expanded exhibition facilities, including those available to selected Members, who in the words of the founders 'may offer their performances to public inspection, and acquire that degree of reputation and encouragement which they shall be deemed to deserve'. The RA Schools have continued to attract gifted students who are skilfully and conscientiously enabled to pursue their own artistic bent without prescriptive hindrance from unimaginative tutors and without having to pay any fees. In the beautiful Library research activity has reached new heights of unpretentious historical and scholarly excellence. RA Publications has a highly successful, varied list, and the RA Magazine reaches out to a vast readership of the Friends (set up by Hugh Casson in the early 1980s) and beyond.

The Academy is, I dare say without fear of contradiction, more alive and more important to our national life than it has ever been. This is, without question, a function of its unique composition: it is a broadly democratic body of artists who have been elected by their fellow artists in recognition of their quality and significance as artists. Much depends, of course on the quality of the electing body and of its leadership, and the great change that has been effected in the Academy's standing is in part a function of a membership that has itself changed over the years, in a process that began in earnest in the early 1970s and which gathered pace through the next 20 years.

Painter academicians were at first slow to respond to the spirit of change, but un-academic printmaker Members such as the mercurial Michael Rothenstein, the pioneering genius of direct printing, realised that lively younger painters who worked also in other media – artists like Joe Tilson, Allen Jones and Tom Phillips – might be brought into the Academy under the categorical rubric of 'printmakers'. All three were elected thus in the early 1980s. The usefulness of this catch-all device persisted: in 1996, Christopher Le Brun, a painter and sculptor of distinction, and now PRA, was elected as such, and in 2011, so was Grayson Perry. The make-up of the Academy changed as each small new wave of contemporary practitioners sought the election of artists they knew and respected. John Hoyland[7], Gillian Ayres, Paul Huxley, Terry Frost and Albert Irvin, among the very best abstract painters of their generation, joined the Academy in the 1990s as did Patrick Caulfield, the greatest figurative stylist of his time. William Tucker and Phillip King, leaders of Bryan Robertson's 'New Generation', were elected in these years, to be joined at last in 2002 by Sir Anthony Caro, their own mentor, who in 1972 had declined Kneale's invitation to 'British Sculpture' on anti-Academy principle.

As the century turned the next generation of experimental and 'conceptual' sculptors joined them: Richard Long, Bill Woodrow, Richard Deacon, Tony Cragg, as have gifted artists of the generation that caused a great sensation, though not necessarily in the exhibition that took that word as its title: Gary Hume, Gillian Wearing, Michael Landy, Tracey Emin, Tacita Dean and others. These have been joined in recent years by Honorary Academicians of international distinction, among them

7 In 1967 John Hoyland, at 33, the most ambitious abstract artist of the 'new generation', had filled the Whitechapel Gallery twice over in the course of his astonishing exhibition of huge colour-field paintings; only seven years earlier at the Academy Schools, the PRA, Sir Charles Wheeler, an old-fashioned figurative sculptor, had angrily ordered Hoyland's Diploma exhibition of Pollock-like abstractions to be taken off the walls.
8 Michael Craig-Martin is quoted from an interview in the *Guardian*, 25 June 2012.
9 'There is no shortage…' I have forgotten the name of the artist who said this.

Ed Ruscha, Jeff Koons, Anselm Kiefer, Mimmo Paladino and Frank Gehry. Their presence in this exhibition testifies to their commitment.

And so it goes. Times have indeed changed. The Academy is transformed. This extraordinary sea change over a mere 40 years into something rich, and what would have seemed to the mid-century gentlemen of the Academy decidedly strange, is spectacularly evidenced in the present show. This is the RA now. Whatever else it does, it demonstrates, above all, the redundancy of the old – and surviving – categories of membership. As Michael Craig-Martin (elected as a 'painter' in 2006) has put it: 'Any creative person has more options than you could possibly deal with. The problem of the artist is to eliminate most of them.'[8] In this present exhibition we are invited to look at works of enormous diversity. Whatever they may or may not do in the 'traditional' forms, in the modern Academy its artists might do anything else they feel inclined to do: 'architects' make prints and paintings; 'painters' make films, videos, photographic works and installations; 'sculptors' take walks and photographs, make architectural interventions, create images out of postcards, explode garden sheds and photograph snake fangs; printmakers make paintings and sculptures, constructions and pots. The time has surely come for the Academy to elect to its membership 'artists' *tout court*: it is the *Royal Academy of Arts*.

And when the move into the newly transformed premises in Burlington Gardens is finally achieved, through the generosity of those others who will surely be encouraged by that of the Academicians themselves, then there is every hope that its many activities will continue to flourish and expand. For the 'arts' comprehend music, poetry and dance, and there will be rooms and opportunities, it is to be hoped, for these to find a place in the renovated Academy of the new century. Change the context, change the text; new spaces call forth new uses of space, new possibilities of presentation. 'There is no shortage of ideas,' said a wise artist, 'only a shortage of places to put them.'[9] 6 Burlington Gardens, its frontage decorated by statues of the great thinkers of European civilised thought and action, will provide such places, and the Academy will there consolidate its recently acquired centrality to the national culture.

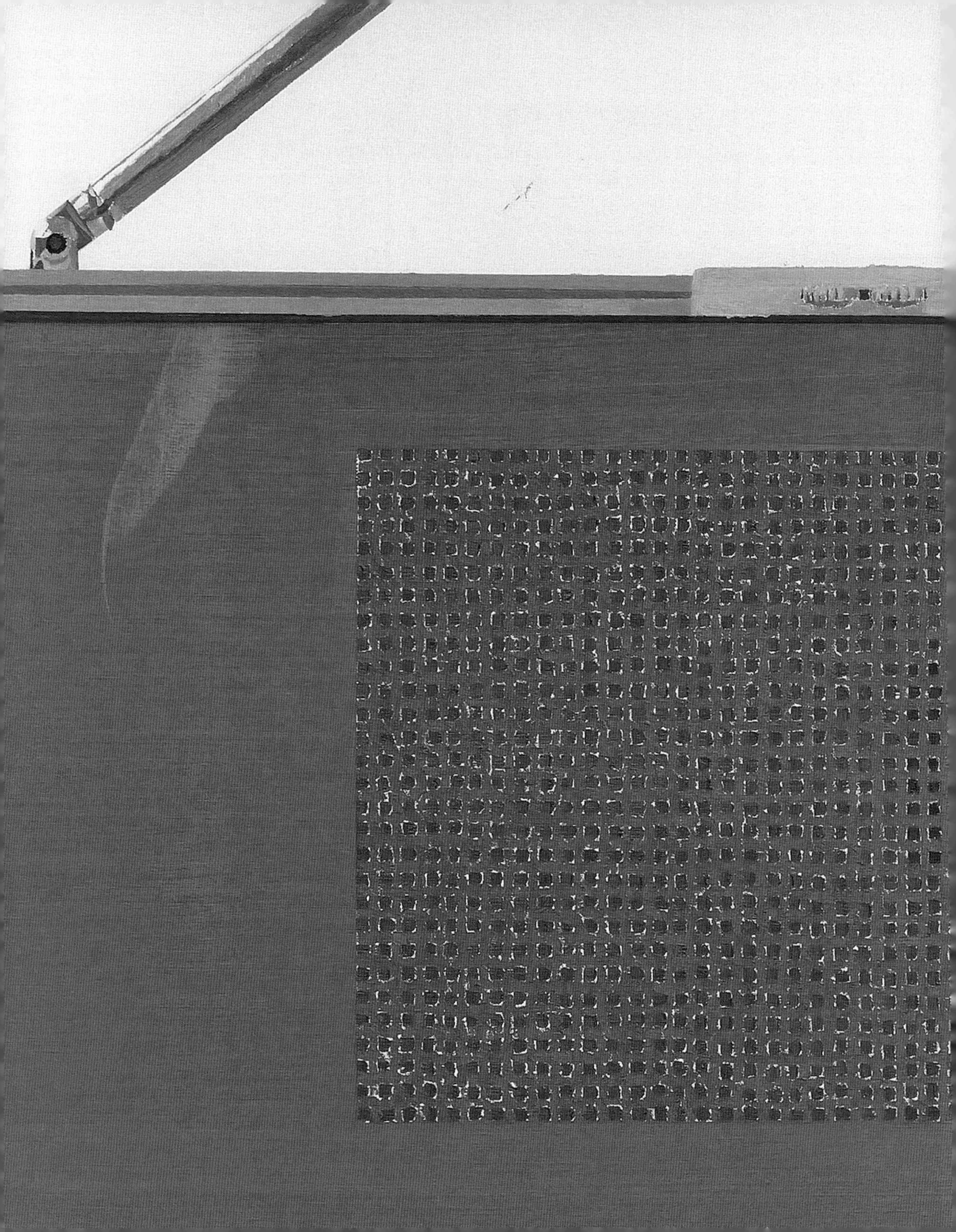

Ivor Abrahams RA

Born: 10 January 1935, Wigan, Lancashire, UK
Elected ARA: 31 May 1989
Elected RA: 26 June 1991
Category of Membership: Sculptor

Ivor Abrahams has had a well-travelled artistic career. A student of Anthony Caro at St Martin's School of Art, and of Karel Vogel at Camberwell School of Art in the mid-1950s, Abrahams went on to apprentice at the Fiorini Art bronze foundry. After a period of inspirational travel throughout Europe, he began an academic career that has taken in positions at Goldsmiths College of Art, the Royal College of Art and the Slade School of Art, culminating in his Professorship of Sculpture at the Royal Academy Schools (2007–10). Abrahams now splits his time between England and France.

An exhibitor in the landmark '22 Young Sculptors' exhibition at the Institute of Contemporary Arts in 1961, Abrahams cemented his international reputation with a show at the Kolnisher Kunstverein, Cologne, in 1973. He has gone on to have numerous solo shows throughout Europe and the United States, including a major retrospective at the Yorkshire Sculpture Park in 1984. His work over five decades has moved in and out of figuration. He is currently still working on architectural cityscape structures and is revisiting the famous garden sculptures of the 1970s, after a successful showing of this body of work at the Henry Moore Institute in 2008.

This whimsical mixed media work demonstrates Abrahams' unabashed commitment to accessible work, and a recurrent interest in the human form and its interaction with the natural world. The female figure is sensually drawn with a sculptor's sense of line and of almost monumental stasis within a dynamic scene, coloured by passionate foreground and background strokes. Uplifting and optimistic, the work expresses a universal feeling of emotional climax and release.

Butterfly Lady, 2011
Mixed media
63 × 51 cm

Marina Abramović Hon RA

Born: 30 November 1946, Belgrade, in former Yugoslavia
Elected Honorary RA: 27 September 2011

Marina Abramović describes herself as the 'grandmother of performance art'. Over her 40-year career she has transformed and redefined the genre with her provocative, compelling and highly original practice. Continually experimental, Abramović has used both her body and her audience as her medium and subject, testing and exploring not only the boundaries of art but also the limits of human mental and physical endurance. She has exhibited at major institutions across the globe including the Manchester International Festival (2009), Guggenheim Museum, New York, (2005), Museum of Modern Art, Oxford, (1995), Centre Georges Pompidou, Paris, 1990, Neue National Galerie, Berlin (1993) and the Venice Biennale (1976, 1997). She has received many diverse and prestigious accolades including the Golden Lion for Best Artist for her video installation/performance piece *Balkan Baroque* (1997). Her work was the subject of a retrospective at The Museum of Modern Art, New York in 2010, and plans for the Marina Abramović Institute, a performance space and training centre, were unveiled earlier this year.

In her last UK solo show at the Lisson Gallery, Abramović exhibited a series of large-scale, high-resolution photographs – a new medium for the artist. Although stilled, they are characteristically visually arresting and highly theatrical. *Holding the Lamb* presents a scene that, with its biblical connotations of sacrifice, mercy and willpower, connects to her deeply personal performance work. It also describes a paradox: despite her triumphant stance, her mortality is reinforced by her sublime surroundings. It is perhaps portraying internal indecision; maybe she is waiting for a sign from something more powerful than herself. Abramović has reflected that her relationship to a dominant 'other' has been significant in her life: 'On one side is this strict orthodox religion, on the other is communism, and I am this little girl pulled between the two. It makes me who I am.'

Holding the Lamb, 2010
Colour pigment print
162.7 × 202.7 cm

Norman Ackroyd RA

Born: 26 March 1938, Leeds, Yorkshire, UK
Elected ARA: 4 May 1988
Elected RA: 26 June 1991
Category of Membership: Engraver

One of Britain's foremost landscape artists, Norman Ackroyd attended the Leeds College of Art and the Royal College of Art in London, where he studied under Julian Trevelyan. Subsequently he lived for several years in the United States. He was appointed Professor of Etching, University of the Arts, in 1994 and a Senior Fellow of the Royal College of Art in 2000, and in 2007 was made CBE for services to Engraving and Printing. His work is held in many prominent public collections including the British Museum, Tate, The Museum of Modern Art, New York, National Gallery, Washington DC and Amsterdam Rijksmuseum. He has completed numerous mural commissions, notably for Lloyds Bank, London; British Airways, Birmingham Airport; the British Embassy in Moscow and Lazards Bank, Stratton Street, London. Most recently he visited the Galapagos Islands and produced a mural for the Sainsbury Laboratories for

Plant Development at the University of Cambridge. He has also collaborated with poets, most recently publishing *A Line in the Water* (2009) with Douglas Dunn.

Ackroyd's love of landscape was nurtured on long boyhood bicycle rides in the Yorkshire Dales, and has since developed into extensive travels across the British Isles producing the lyrical landscape works that have formed the backbone of his career. This painting features the uninhabited island in the St Kilda archipelago in the north Atlantic, which Ackroyd first explored in the 1970s. His knowledge and profound respect for the outdoors is clear in his subtle use of colour and gesture to evoke his elusive and variable subject. Whether on a large or intimate scale, in watercolour, etching, bronze or oils, as in this painting, Ackroyd's work brings energy and freshness to the genre.

St Kilda, Boreray, 2012
Oil on canvas
60.9 × 76.2 cm

Will Alsop RA

Born: 12 December 1947, Northampton, UK
Elected RA: 18 May 2000
Category of Membership: Architect

Will Alsop studied at the Northampton School of Art and the Architectural Association. He established his own practice in 1981, originally in partnership with John Lyall and later with Jan Störmer. Projects include the Cardiff Bay Visitor Centre, the Ben Pimlott Building (Goldsmiths, University of London) and the Clarke Quay Redevelopment Project (Singapore). Alsop's practice has won numerous awards including RIBA regional and national awards and the Stirling Prize in 2000 for Peckham Library. He has held many academic posts at institutions including the Vienna University of Technology and the Universities of London and Hanover. He was also a tutor of sculpture at Central St Martins College of Art and Design. Alsop's practice, ALL Design, currently has offices in London, Chongqing and Toronto. He was awarded an OBE and in July 2007 he received an honorary Doctorate of Civil Law (DCL) from the University of East Anglia.

Painting is always Alsop's first creative step towards a building's design as he uses it to challenge and explore the ideas that will become material substance. In *Quendo* the importance of line, instilled in Alsop during his time at art school under Henry Bird, is strongly evident. There is also a typical emphasis on experimentation; he is particularly inventive with colour and in his exploration of unusual shape. The vibrant and playful diagonal gestures are exuberant, and create not only dynamism within the composition but also a sense of liberty. Incorporating unbounded, uncontrived forms that appear to be escaping from the pre-conceived rectangular border reflects Alsop's respect for the imagination and his willingness to challenge conservative orthodoxy. 'I have never seen an ugly blob,' he has said. Spontaneous, abstract form has an inherent beauty and freedom that he tries to incorporate into his building designs, thus bringing innovation to architecture by transcending its traditional relationship with structure, function and construction.

Quendo, 2011
Mixed media
120.5 × 150 cm

Diana Armfield RA

Born: 11 June 1920, Ringwood, Hampshire, UK
Elected ARA: 1 June 1989
Elected RA: 26 June 1991
Category of Membership: Painter

Diana Armfield studied at the Slade School of Fine Art and Central School of Arts and Crafts. She taught at the Byam Shaw School of Art from 1959 and was an Artist-in-Residence in Perth, Australia, in 1985, and in Jackson, Wyoming, USA, in 1989. Her most recent solo exhibition was held by Browse & Darby, London, in 2010 to celebrate her 90th birthday. She is a Member of the Royal Watercolour Society, the Royal West of England Academy, the Royal Cambrian Society (Hon Retired) and an Honorary Member of the Pastel Society and the New English Art Club. In addition, her work features in many public collections, including those of the National Trust, HRH The Prince of Wales and the Contemporary Art Society, Wales.

Armfield began her career designing wallpaper and textiles, and evidence of this still remains on show at the Victoria and Albert Museum. In 1965, however, she turned to painting. Married to Bernard Dunstan RA, they are both painters of light. She says of herself: 'I work from observation and experience; draw and paint what I can admire, enjoy or love; to share with others what I discover and reflect on. I hope to reveal and confirm that the things and experiences I paint are of lasting importance and enormously worth cherishing. To translate into paint is always a challenge and something of a mystery.'

This oil painting is typical of her style, and the variety of brush strokes – from the thick marks in the sky and foreground to the more delicate ones used for the distant roofs and the figure and dog – show her dedication to the act of painting. Landscapes, café scenes and flowers as 'still-life' are often her subject of choice, and this Italian view painted in pastel colours presents a charming impressionistic scene.

The Walk Below San Gimignano, 2010
Oil on canvas
23.5 × 20.3 cm

Gillian Ayres RA

Born: 3 February 1930, London, UK
Elected ARA: 5 May 1982
Elected RA: 29 May 1991
Category of Membership: Painter

Gillian Ayres studied at Camberwell School of Art. She became Head of Painting at Winchester School of Art (1978–81), and has taught at both St Martin's School of Art and the Royal College of Art. Her work has featured in many key group shows, including the Whitechapel Gallery's seminal 'British Painting in the '60s' (1965), and a retrospective of her work was held at the Serpentine Gallery, London, in 1983. More recently she has had solo shows at Tate Britain (1995) and the Royal Academy of Arts (1997). She was awarded an OBE in 1986.

Ayres has said: 'It's all I ever wanted to do, all my life. I can't live long enough to paint all I want to do. Thirty years ago, I gave up my teaching job at Winchester to paint. And that's what I do.' She uses a distinctive visual language to create bright, vibrant and abstract paintings that are 'about painting, about shape and colour, not telling stories'.

The shape of the canvas is key to the artist's work, for it both contains and emphasises the decorative and individual aesthetic of the forms and marks within. Ayres has a respect and instinctive sensibility for the material substances involved in painting, which is reflected in the fact that a 'cartouche' – the title of this painting – is not only an oblong used to bear a design or inscription, but is also associated with the protective oval outline that was used in ancient Egypt whenever a Pharaoh's name was inscribed. This piece also reveals her unwavering belief that painting is still a primary mode of modern creative expression, that it can 'reference reality, yet it is also able to represent an imaginative vision that has never been seen before'. Ayres believes that a verbal analysis of painting can never parallel the experience of looking or making; her work speaks for itself.

Cartouche 1, 2001
Oil on canvas
129.1 cm oval

Phyllida Barlow RA

Born: 4 April 1944, Newcastle-upon-Tyne, UK
Elected RA: 26 May 2011
Category of Membership: Sculptor

Phyllida Barlow studied at Chelsea College of Art and the Slade School of Art in London before going on to teach at both. Until recently she was Professor of Fine Art and Director of Undergraduate Studies at the Slade. In 2010 she had a critically acclaimed two-person show with Nairy Baghramian at the Serpentine Gallery, London. She has since participated in many group and solo exhibitions around the world, and her drawings were shown at the Henry Moore Institute earlier this year.

Barlow has become known for her large-scale installations, usually constructed on-site and from inexpensive, disposable materials such as cardboard, cement, polystyrene, plywood and fabric. Inspired by everyday urban objects and city life, she would 'love to be able to achieve in my work the mutability of the man-made environment, with its growing and decaying – the roadworks, the buildings coming down and going up – and the natural world, which is doing the same in tandem'.

Visually and spatially imposing, Barlow's sculptures are, as she says, 'sensations of physicality'. They satirise the idea of monumentality, which she sees as faintly absurd because 'so often we don't know what the monument is. We've lived through a decade where we've seen it literally topple in front of our eyes.'

Drawing has always been a continuous part of Barlow's practice, as it is a key way in which she develops and records ideas. She calls them 'bad copies'; they are derived from the environment, but are never drawn from life. As in her sculptures, these drawings explore texture, colour and form to create highly original, exuberant works of art.

Untitled: Bolsters Trestles 1, 2011
Acrylic on watercolour paper
60.5 × 78 cm

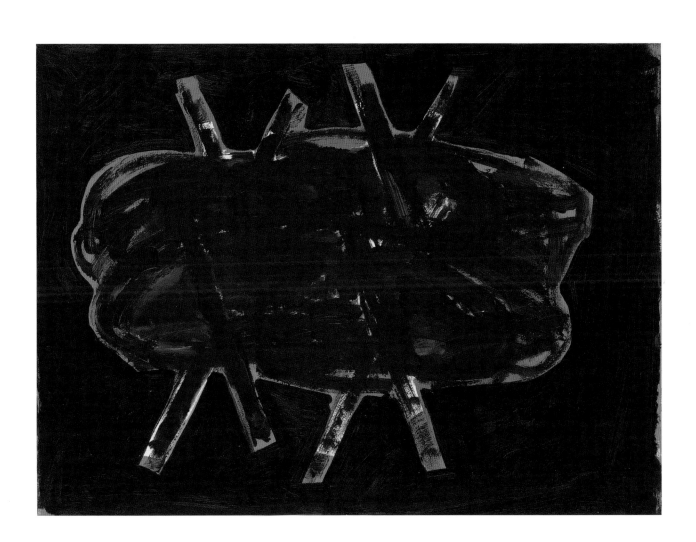

Basil Beattie RA

Born: 9 January 1935, West Hartlepool, County Durham, UK
Elected RA: 2 June 2006
Category of Membership: Painter

Basil Beattie studied at West Hartlepool College of Art and the Royal Academy Schools, and taught at Goldsmiths College from the 1960s to the '90s. He has twice been shortlisted for the Jerwood Prize and once for the Charles Wollaston Award, and was a prizewinner of the John Moores in 1989. In 2007 a selection of his work from Tate's collection was displayed at Tate Britain and he has recently shown in London at Purdy Hicks Gallery and James Hyman Fine Art. In 2011 a book entitled *Taking Steps* was published, representing 25 years of his work.

Beattie's first exposure to Abstract Expressionism at Tate and the Whitechapel Gallery in the late 1950s/early 1960s inspired a career distinguished by a sensuous and physical use of paint. Developing a repertoire of metaphorical language has combined this interest with an understanding of the narrative power of implicit imagery. The signs and symbols –

usually architectural motifs, such as doors, stairways and tunnels – allow him to fuse both 'the process and materiality with thoughts about how we read things and how we relate them to our experiences'.

In 2006 Beattie embarked upon the *Janus* series of paintings, to which *Far and Away* belongs. Janus, the Roman God depicted as having two faces with one looking to the past and one to the future, presides over transitions, beginnings and endings, entrances and exits. The series features vertical units often framing a series of perspectival horizons, with suggestions of travel and journeys. The units resemble rear-view mirrors or windscreens, suggesting both past and future, and evoke Beattie's desire to look both back and forward. By retaining the importance of the gesture, colour and scale of his past work and then combining it with new imagery and ambition, *Far and Away* is a perfect expression of this paradoxical desire.

Far and Away (Janus series), 2010
Oil and wax on canvas
213 × 198 cm

John Bellany RA

Born: 18 June 1942, Port Seton, East Lothian, Scotland, UK
Elected ARA: 20 November 1986
Elected RA: 26 June 1991
Category of Membership: Painter

John Bellany studied painting at Edinburgh College of Art and the Royal College of Art, London. His work has been included in many key group exhibitions both nationally and internationally since 1963, and he has had solo shows at the Scottish National Gallery of Modern Art, Edinburgh, the National Portrait Gallery, and the Serpentine Gallery, London. A retrospective at the National Galleries of Scotland will open this November.

Bellany first became known in the 1970s for his compositions of symbolic figures and objects that were not afraid of embracing grand themes, such as good and evil, life and death. He consciously allied himself with the northern tradition of Hieronymous Bosch and Pieter Brueghel, and developed a vivid expressionist style reminiscent of Edvard Munch and Max Beckmann.

Renewed after major surgery in the 1980s, Bellany's palette brightened as he found fresh subjects in flowers and travel, writing to an old friend in capitals: 'COLOUR IS THE MOST IMPORTANT THING.' Of Italy, where he lives and works for some of the year (and the setting of this painting), he has said: 'The landscape, the climate, the warmth of the people – everything has tended to make me take a gentler view of life and that's bound to be reflected in the work. The stress and strain of contemporary life just drops away… It's changed the tone of appreciation of what could happen after death, if anything. These thoughts go through my mind all the time when I'm painting – as a result I have a much more optimistic view.'

Domenica, 2012
Oil on canvas
122 × 122 cm

Gordon Benson RA

Born: 5 October 1944, Glasgow, Scotland, UK
Elected RA: 18 May 2000
Category of Membership: Architect

Studying at the Architectural Association compounded Gordon Benson's belief that the best architectural design synthesises poetic meaning with social utility. In the mid-1980s he formed his current architectural practice, Benson + Forsyth. Controversially for the time, it combined the more successful aspects of Le Corbusier's urbanism with elements of Georgian and Victorian architectural models to form a unique brand of social architecture. The firm won its first major public building commission in 1991, the extension for the Museum of Scotland, and the success of this project led to it being chosen to design the extension for the National Gallery of Ireland, completed in 2000.

In 1992 the prefecture of Toyama, North West of Japan, asked seven European architects to design buildings in its fourteen towns that would explore the notion of progress and the passage of time, and provide a commentary on their culture. Aiming to bring fresh understanding to the known by defamiliarising the habitual, Benson + Forsyth's design selectively and critically juxtaposes traditional and contemporary concerns. Within the structure is a wall that divides east and west: contemporary Japan, symbolised in steel, concrete and timber, from ancient agrarian customs, represented by a traditional basket constructed of timber, bamboo and ninth-century knots. This section of the building is thatched with rice grass, which is also grown in a circle around the pavilion. The building itself is a sundial – working out where the shadows would fall, the line of the sun on the solstice was cast into the concrete. Also within the wall is a stairway placed directly on Oshima's meridian, which ascends to a cube within which there is the recording of a human heartbeat, a biological register of time. Embodied in this sensitively executed and researched building is Benson's conviction that architecture is able to engage intelligently with its physical and temporal location to create something of cultural significance.

The Divided House, Oshima, Japan, 1993
Photograph and pen
61 × 61 cm

Tony Bevan RA

Born: 12 July 1951, Bradford, Yorkshire, UK
Elected RA: 27 March 2007
Category of Membership: Painter

Tony Bevan studied at the Bradford School of Art, then in London at Goldsmiths College and the Slade School of Fine Art. His work exists in many prominent international collections, including The Museum of Contemporary Art, Los Angeles, The Metropolitan Museum of Art, New York, the National Portrait Gallery and Tate.

Throughout Bevan's oeuvre there is a unifying aesthetic that derives from his use of charcoal and self-produced acrylic paints. He likes to fix his work to the floor, allowing him to force pigment into the pores of the paper or canvas. Strong, thick lines define skeletal forms, whether it is landscape, architectural structures, or the human figure. However, it is the isolated human head, specifically his own,

that has been Bevan's most obsessive subject since the 1990s.

Bevan acknowledges that these portraits are not 'so much to do with the face as with the head as a whole, and the neck, tendons, vessels and nerves that connect it to the body. It's the vulnerability that interests me.' It is tempting to describe the saturated red lines that delineate the head in *Self-portrait* as tendons or wounds. Bevan, however, prefers to talk of them as 'flow patterns', deliberately avoiding any reference to either internal or external structures, and thereby eschewing any Cartesian notions of the mind/body divide. Psychologically imposing, Bevan's portraits expose an uncompromisingly raw vision of human experience.

Self-portrait, 2012
Charcoal and acrylic on canvas
107 × 108 cm

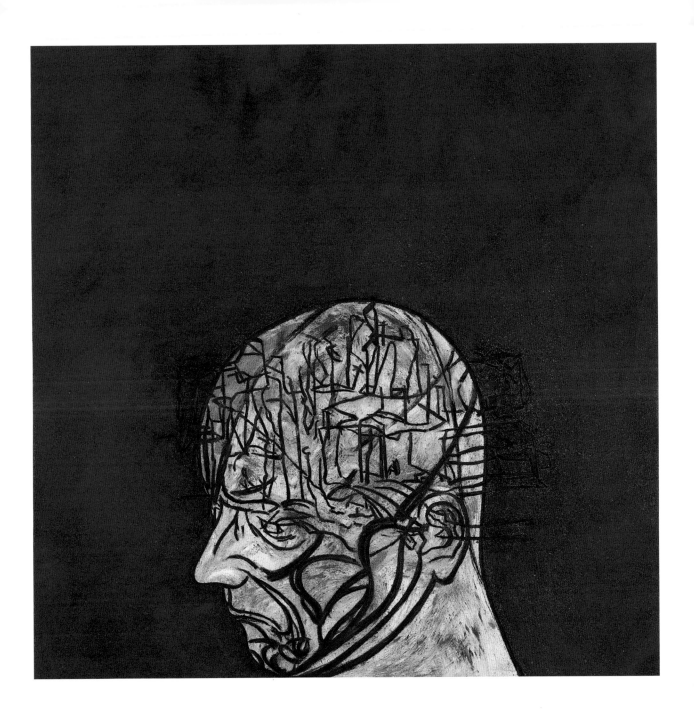

Elizabeth Blackadder RA

Born: 24 September 1931, Falkirk, Stirlingshire, Scotland, UK
Elected ARA: 22 April 1971
Elected RA: 29 April 1976
Category of Membership: Painter

Having completed her studies at Edinburgh University and Edinburgh College of Art in 1955, Elizabeth Blackadder was awarded a Carnegie Travelling Scholarship to Europe and she studied in Italy for nine months. After marrying the painter John Houston the following year, she settled in Scotland and held teaching posts at the Edinburgh College of Art from 1962 to 1986. Although receiving numerous commissions and recognition for her stained glass, lithographs and tapestries, it was for her meticulous watercolours that she became increasingly recognised. Blackadder's first solo exhibition was held at 57 Gallery, Edinburgh, in 1959 and since then she has exhibited extensively both in Britain and abroad.

Well-known for her characteristic depiction of still-lifes, Blackadder draws on a wide and varied array of objects carefully chosen and spaced out before her on the table in her studio. Fascinated by colour and pattern in a manner not dissimilar to Matisse or Bonnard, she uses objects that attract the viewer and displays them with an often quizzical sense of spatial ambiguity.

In the 1980s Blackadder visited Japan and from this point on one is able to see the influence, not only on her style but also through the introduction of objects obtained on these travels, such as the dish shown here. This, alongside the selection of boxes, candles and an artichoke heart, is presented as a relic from her travels, and we are able to sense the personal affection with which she depicts her carefully considered subjects. They are not scattered idly, but are each placed with an important role to play within the structure and harmony of the composition, holding meaning to the artist and an elusive attraction to the viewer.

Table with Boxes, Candles and a Japanese Dish, 2012
Oil on canvas
50.8 × 60.9 cm

Olwyn Bowey RA

Born: 10 February 1936, Stockton-on-Tees, Durham, UK
Elected ARA: 24 April 1970
Elected RA: 24 April 1975
Category of Membership: Painter

Olwyn Bowey is a First Class alumnus of the Royal College of Art, where she received a continuation scholarship and a David Murray Landscape Scholarship. Her initial interests began in portraiture, before she discovered her passion for landscape, still-life and in particular the tradition of the artist-plantsman. An exhibition of drawings exploring this theme was held in the Royal Academy's Friends' Room in 2000.

Bowey's greenhouse in Sussex doubles as her studio, and a love of plants and rural life pervades her work. Such is her passion for the natural world that Bowey says she 'really wanted to be a naturalist and a botanist, rather than a painter'. A visit to a friend's house in West Sussex sparked her imagination and her move away from London into a cottage on an estate. Yet despite her studied attention to flora, her response is consistently emotional rather than scientific.

Demonstrating her characteristically expressive ease with oils, this still-life also has a mood of lively intimacy that draws in the viewer. We sense the rough and smooth of the earthenware, dappled verdant light on the pink and purple hues of the English foxgloves, and most particularly Bowey's warm and impressionistic interest in her subject.

The Lucky MoneyToad, 2012
Oil on board
76.2 × 61 cm

Frank Bowling RA

Born: 29 February 1936, Guyana
Elected RA: 25 May 2005
Category of Membership: Painter

Frank Bowling graduated from the Royal College of Art in 1962. Since the mid-1960s he has travelled and maintained his exhibition career between his New York and London studios. His paintings have been widely shown internationally, including solo exhibitions at the Whitney Museum of American Art (1971), the Serpentine Gallery (1986) and a UK touring retrospective 'Bowling through the Century' in 1996–8. His paintings are also exhibited in many permanent collections including Tate and the Victoria and Albert Museum in London, The Metropolitan Museum, the Museum of Modern Art and the Whitney Museum in New York.

Much of his early work was figurative, but when Bowling moved to New York in 1966 he started to concentrate on abstract pictorial issues relating to colour and composition. He left his easel behind and began to use more unconventional methods, pinning his canvases to his studio walls and floor and applying paint though movements of spilling, dripping and brushing. It was during this period that Bowling was to find a style that remains recognisable to this day. Alive with high-key, lyrical colour, his paintings are created through acts of spontaneity and chance.

GreenChinaGate displays his trademark experimentation with texture and the emotive potential of colours, which he says communicate 'a visual experience of uniquely sensuous immediacy'. Bowling explains: 'It all happens very much in an extempore way. I don't have any pre-planned idea about how I'm going to make a painting.' The fluid bands of colour in this work are typical of Bowling's paintings, and are governed by feeling and touch. 'Something happens with the material through the process, and these amazing and beautiful things appear.' In *GreenChinaGate* we can see the artist's attempt to capture these elusive moments.

GreenChinaGate, 2010
Acrylic on paper
46.6 × 50.8 cm

William Bowyer RA

Born: 25 May 1926, Leek, Staffordshire, UK
Elected ARA: 25 April 1974
Elected RA: 24 March 1981
Category of Membership: Painter

William Bowyer trained at Burslem School of Art and then the Royal College of Art where his tutors included Carel Weight and Ruskin Spear. He later became Head of Fine Art at Maidstone College of Art. He is a Member of the Royal Watercolour Society, the Royal Society of Portrait Painters and the New English Art Club, and his work can be seen at the National Portrait Gallery, London. Recent solo exhibitions were held at Fosse Gallery, Gloucestershire (2008) and the Chappel Galleries, Essex (2009).

Bowyer's work belongs in the category of English figurative painting and he has been greatly influenced by Constable and Turner. His subject-matter, predominantly landscape paintings but also portraits and cricket scenes, tell us about his life. As fellow Academician Ken Howard commented: 'Bill Bowyer's work communicates with us directly. It gives us a way of seeing the world, and above all it is life-enhancing.'

Bowyer is captivated by Walberswick in Suffolk, where he spends much of his time, but this evocative coastal scene is in Dorset. Initially, viewers are enchanted by the warm haze of colours but the distant lighthouse creates a focal point, a reminder that this is a real place where they too can visit.

Low Tide, Dorset, 1974
Watercolour
44 × 74 cm

James Butler RA

Born: 25 July 1931, London, UK
Elected ARA: 24 April 1964
Elected RA: 15 June 1972
Category of Membership: Sculptor

James Butler trained at Maidstone School of Art and then St Martin's School of Art and the Royal College of Art in London. He spent ten years as a professional stone carver, and worked for a number of years creating sculpture for the Royal Shakespeare Company's productions. He later taught at City & Guilds of London Art School as well as the Royal Academy Schools. He has received many commissions for public artworks that can be seen around the world, including a twice-life-sized portrait of President Kenyatta, in Nairobi; Field Marshal Earl Alexander of Tunis, at Wellington Barracks, London; and a memorial statue of King Richard III, in Castle Gardens, Leicester. He has also completed a number of designs for the Royal Mint.

Butler is known for his spirited sculptures of carefree children, as well as dancers, female nudes and virtuosic portrait busts. He has also created a number of moving war memorials, notably *The Rainbow Division Memorial* shown in the courtyard of the Royal Academy last summer. Deeply sympathetic, it is perhaps informed by Butler's own National Service experience.

A strong technical understanding of the sculptural process supports all of these diverse projects. His portrait heads are sculpted first from clay, which Butler uses because it is 'a wonderfully expressive material and faithfully records the movement of the sculptor's hands'. A mould is then made from this, which is then cast in bronze. Using a solution of salts and acids, the surface is then patinated to give the subtle colour range that we can see on the finished sculpture. Despite the permanence of bronze the sculpture retains immediacy and life.

Portrait of a Girl, 2001
Bronze casting on a black marble base (edition 1/4)
Height 35 cm

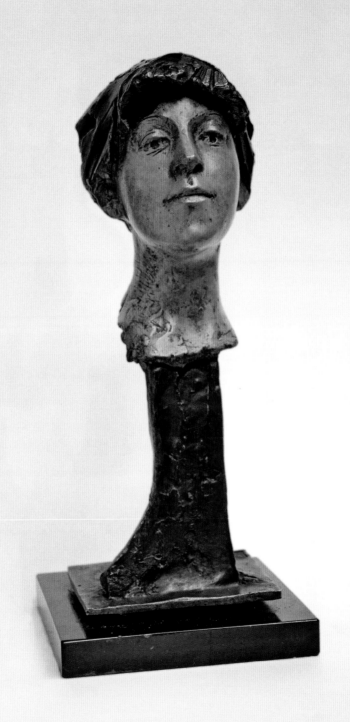

Jeffery Camp RA

Born: 17 April 1923, Oulton Broad, Suffolk, UK
Elected ARA: 26 April 1974
Elected RA: 9 May 1984
Category of Membership: Painter

Jeffery Camp studied at Lowestoft and Ipswich Schools of Art, and later at the Edinburgh College of Art. He went on to teach at Chelsea School of Art and the Slade School of Art in London. His first solo exhibitions were held at the Beaux-Arts Gallery, London, in 1959 and subsequent solo shows were held at New Art Centre, a retrospective at the South London Art Gallery, the Serpentine Gallery, Nigel Greenwood Gallery, Browse & Darby and Art Space Gallery/Michael Richardson Contemporary Art, the gallery which now represents him. He was a Phillips Prize-winner in 1965 and he won the Wollaston Award in 1996 for the most distinguished work in the Royal Academy's 'Summer Exhibition'.

For over 50 years Camp has used his paintings to convey the sensation and excitement of being in spaces where land, water and sky meet. His poetic swirls of colour are at once lyrical and delicate.

Nothing is insignificant in his eyes. He sweeps through varying compositions; his capacity to find interest in his subject is expressed through passionate brushwork and his feeling for weight of colour.

'A painter's work', Camp wrote, 'may change less in the middle years and explode with surprises at the end.' In this recent explosion the surprise is the stillness of the Moon, around which the circular rhythms revolve. The paint is loose and suggestive as Camp pushes and pulls, strokes and dabs the pigment to create a shimmering surface and reflections for the diver to plummet into.

Encountering Camp's recent canvases for the first time, Timothy Hyman RA wrote: 'My immediate response is that they are some kind of summation: all the experiences of a lifetime have come to be embedded within this imagery.'

Moon, 2012
Oil on canvas
152.4 × 152.4 cm

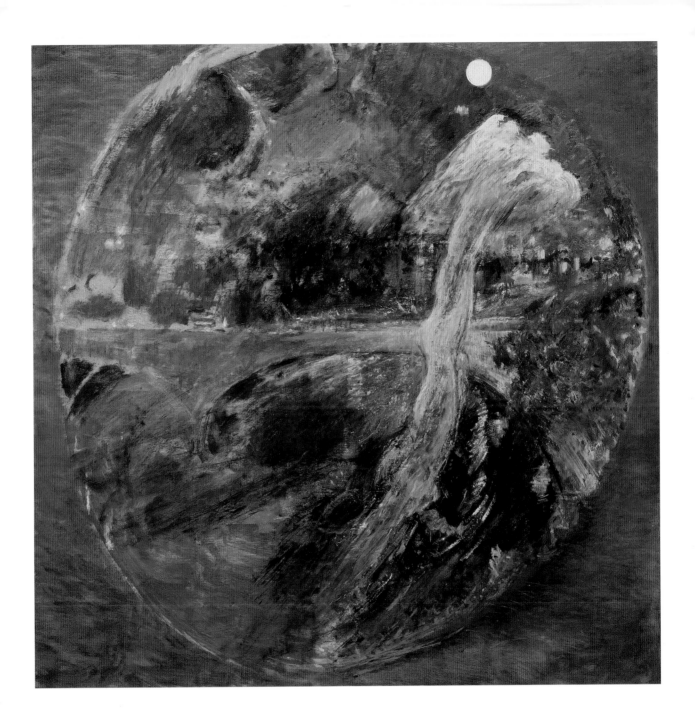

Anthony Caro RA

Born: 8 March 1924, New Malden, Surrey, UK
Elected RA: 9 March 2004
Category of Membership: Sculptor

Anthony Caro has played a pivotal role in the development of twentieth-century sculpture. After studying sculpture at the Royal Academy Schools in London he worked as assistant to Henry Moore. He came to public attention with a show at the Whitechapel Gallery in 1963, where he exhibited large abstract sculptures brightly painted and standing directly on the ground so that they engaged the spectator on a one-to-one basis. This was a radical departure from the way sculpture had hitherto been seen, and paved the way for future developments in three-dimensional art.

Caro's teaching at St Martin's School of Art in London (1953–81) was very influential. His questioning approach opened up new possibilities, both formally and with regard to subject-matter. His innovative work, as well as his teaching, led to a flowering and a new confidence in sculpture worldwide.

Major exhibitions include retrospectives at the Museum of Modern Art, New York (1975), the Trajan Markets, Rome (1992), the Museum of Contemporary Art, Tokyo (1995), Tate Britain (2005), and three museums in Pas-de-Calais, France (2008), to accompany the opening of his Chapel of Light at Bourbourg. He has been awarded many prizes, including the Praemium Imperiale Prize for Sculpture in Tokyo in 1992 and the Lifetime Achievement Award for Sculpture in 1997. He holds many honorary degrees from universities in the UK, USA and Europe. He was knighted in 1987 and received the Order of Merit in May 2000.

Caro often works in steel, but also in a diverse range of other materials including bronze, silver, lead, stoneware, wood and paper. *Fold Centre* dates from 1984 and has an architectural theme, made after a visit to Morocco and seeing the roofs of buildings there.

Fold Centre, 1984
Steel
64.5 × 157.5 × 89 cm

John Carter RA

Born: 3 March 1942, Hampton Hill, Middlesex, UK
Elected RA: 31 May 2007
Category of Membership: Sculptor

John Carter trained at the Twickenham School of Art and Kingston School of Art. He then made a pivotal journey to Italy with a Leverhulme Scholarship; it was here at the British School at Rome that he made his first abstract constructed works. In 1965/6 he worked as an assistant to the sculptor Bryan Kneale. Bryan Robertson invited him to take part in the now-legendary 'New Generations' shows in 'New Generation: 1966' at the Whitechapel Gallery, and that summer the Redfern Gallery asked him to contribute to their summer show, putting his work on the cover of the catalogue. He had his first solo exhibition there two years later. He has since won awards and has had exhibitions and retrospectives in Europe, Japan and the USA. He taught at Chelsea College of Art and Design from 1980 until his retirement in 1999.

Carter's work is intellectually challenging: conceptually grounded in mathematics and both visually clean and abstract, it plays with the boundary between painting and sculpture, constructing a dialogue between flatness and depth. Although classified by the RA as a sculptor, Carter sees his work as 'wall objects', a development of painting.

This work with its descriptive title is typical of Carter's quiet, even austere, minimalist style. He makes a well-defined and calculated plan for a work with clear, incisive, poetic images in a visual language capable of expressing subtleties of thought and imagination. He confesses that he then enjoys the process of achieving the greatest precision in carpentry, construction and painting. His work explores the interaction of knowledge and perception, achieving a quiet harmony.

Superimposed Elements: Horizontal Formation within a Frame, 1991
Acrylic with marble powder on plywood
100 × 200 × 14.8 cm

Stephen Chambers RA

Born: 20 July 1960, London, UK
Elected RA: 13 December 2005
Category of Membership: Printmaker

Stephen Chambers studied at Winchester School of Art and St Martin's School of Art, London, before graduating with a Masters from Chelsea School of Art in 1983. He has won a number of scholarships and awards, including a Rome Scholarship, a Fellowship at Winchester School of Art and a Mark Rothko Memorial Trust Travelling Award. A printmaker and painter, Chambers has also collaborated on three dance projects with the Royal Ballet – 'Sleeping with Audrey' (1996), 'Room of Crooks' (1997, 1999) and 'This House will Burn' (2001), all of which were initiated by and based on his paintings.

According to Chambers his work 'speaks of states of mind, behaviours and sensibilities'.

It hovers between 'abstract and figurative, minimal and decorative' with forms and figures emerging from flat, richly coloured backgrounds.

The Leap from Judas Tree exemplifies Chambers' concern with pared-down forms, flat planes, saturated colour and his trademarks dots and patterns. The patterns cause the painting to almost glisten; they slow the image down and encourage the eye to linger over the details – from the tree to the figure in flight. The unsettling subject (made all the more alarming by there being no glimpse of the ground below) is at odds with the abstract beauty of the shapes and colours. This is a sensual response to a disturbing scenario: 'I don't want to tell you the whole story,' says Chambers.

The Leap from Judas Tree, 2005
Oil on canvas
190 × 160 cm

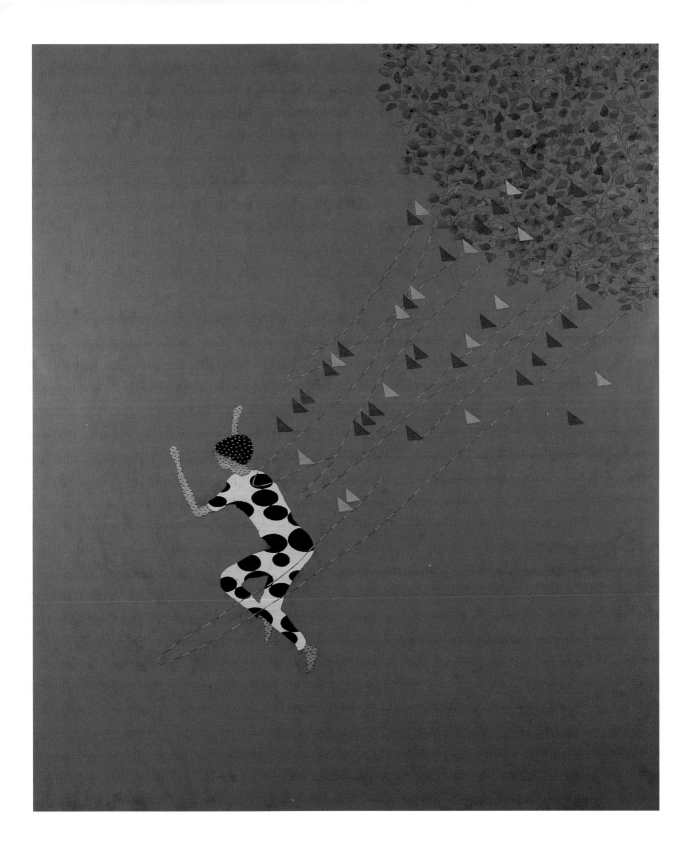

David Chipperfield RA

Born: 18 December 1953, London, UK
Elected RA: 11 December 2007
Category of Membership: Architect

An alumnus of Kingston School of Art and the Architectural Association, London, David Chipperfield worked for architectural leading lights Norman Foster and Richard Rogers before establishing his own practice in 1985, and he now has offices in London, Berlin, Milan and Shanghai.

Chipperfield's designs are a blend of inspiration and pragmatism. His practice philosophy is to 'create specifically detailed buildings that are intimately connected to context and function'. He has won many awards including the Royal Institute of British Architects Stirling Prize in 2007; he was also awarded the Andrea Palladio Prize in 1993 and won the Heinrich Tessenow Gold Medal in 1999. He was made Member of the Florence Academy of Art and Design (2003), an Honorary Fellow of the American Institute of Architects and Honorary Member of the Bund Deutscher Architekten (2007). In 2006 he was appointed Royal Designer for Industry.

The elegance of this drawing is typical of his oeuvre. The architectural aesthetic is minimal and understated: Chipperfield spent many years in Japan and the influence of the country's pared-back design culture is apparent in much of his work. Yet the plan's proportion and scale suggest a self-awareness of the building's importance within a deeply significant and continuing history: the original Neues Museum was damaged during the war and its rebuild was therefore poignant on a social, political and historical level, and as a key German national monument it represented one of the world's largest cultural projects.

Neues Museum, Museum Island, Berlin, Germany, 2009
Mixed media coloured section
70.5 × 140.5 cm

Ann Christopher RA

Born: 4 December 1947, Watford, Hertfordshire, UK
Elected ARA: 21 May 1980
Elected RA: 7 December 1989
Category of Membership: Sculptor

Ann Christopher studied at Harrow School of Art and the West of England College of Art. Her first solo exhibition was in 1969, she was given a retrospective of work in 1989 at the Dorset County Museum and Art Gallery and she has had numerous national and international exhibitions since. She is represented by Pangolin London, and lives and works near Bath.

Part of Christopher's output is site-specific commissions; however, she describes her art as a 'visual diary of her physical and emotional life, an expression of some of the visual experiences stored in my subconscious. Unlike a computer I cannot search and find – the images emerge seemingly at random; it is only once these visual experiences appear in the works that the origins can sometimes be retraced.'

Primarily working in cast bronze, her sculptures can be large or small. She also produces drawings, etchings and photo assemblages. She photographs things that are of current interest to her, such as line and shadow, which she attends to very closely in her sculpture. On her studio wall there is a quotation from the psychoanalytic theorist D. W. Winnicott that asserts: 'It is in the space between inner and outer worlds which is also the space between people – the transitional space – that intimate relationships and creativity occur.'

Christopher's interest in transient and liminal space is evident in *The Edge of Light*. The elegant linearity of the constructed bronze column contrasts with the pale, textured patina of its surface, evoking the natural ruggedness of rock formations. Like the clear shadows that it casts, it has an understated strength and presence without imposing itself on its surroundings.

The Edge of Light, 2002
Bronze (edition 2/5)
Height 220 cm

Geoffrey Clarke RA

Born: 28 November 1924, Darley Dale, Derbyshire, UK
Elected ARA: 24 April 1970
Elected RA: 9 December 1975
Category of Membership: Sculptor

Geoffrey Clarke's artistic trajectory has been unusually varied. He studied at Preston School of Art and Manchester School of Art before serving in the RAF in 1942. He continued his education at Lancaster and Morecambe School of Arts and Crafts and then the Royal College of Art, London (1948–52). Although he was accepted to study Graphic Design, he moved immediately to the Stained Glass department and eventually returned there in 1968 as Head of Light Transmission and Projection Department. Clarke's first solo show was held at Gimpel Fils Gallery, London, in 1952, the same year in which he represented Britain at the Venice Biennale. He has had retrospectives at the Redfern Gallery, the Fine Art Society and Yorkshire Sculpture Park.

Clarke spent his first ten years out of art school on a commission to design 232 square metres of stained glass for Sir Basil Spence's Coventry Cathedral, responding to the biomorphic shapes of Graham Sutherland's famous altarpiece tapestry. Inspired no doubt by this epic project, as well as early Christian signs that he remembers seeing in the British Museum, Clarke's work uses a formal language that alludes to religious and pagan symbols. Moving into sculpture in subsequent years he developed a style that combined craftsmanship with spirituality, evident here in *Baton*; in shape, weight and handling it is reminiscent of early man's tools, such as carved horn or an axe. It also emanates a powerful totem-like presence, but its meaning remains enigmatic and subjective.

Baton, 1989
Bronze (edition 1/2)
Height 48 cm

Robert Clatworthy RA

Born: 31 January 1928, Bridgwater, Somerset, UK
Elected ARA: 25 April 1968
Elected RA: 26 April 1973
Category of Membership: Sculptor

Robert Clatworthy began his training at the West of England College of Art before joining Chelsea School of Art, London, in 1949. In 1951 he studied at the Slade School of Fine Art for a year, after which he enjoyed a varied teaching career at the Royal College of Art, London, the West of England College of Art, St Martin's School of Art and Central School of Art and Design, London. The first of Clatworthy's solo shows were held in 1955 and 1957 at the Hanover Gallery, which represented him originally; his most recent was at the Keith Chapman Gallery, which represents him today. In addition he has featured in many group shows, including 'British Sculpture in the '60s' at Tate Britain in 1965 and 'British Sculptors '72' at the Royal Academy of Arts in 1972. Public commissions in London include *Horseman and Eagle* situated at

Charing Cross Hospital, and *Bull*, commissioned by the GLC for Roehampton.

Clatworthy is usually associated with sculpture but during the 1990s he turned to painting, in particular heads and nudes. His portrayal of animals and people in either medium are powerfully expressed, but Clatworthy prefers not to talk about his art, saying that it 'must stand on its own without the need of words to support it'.

Seated Figure dates from his painting phase and shows his abstract figurative style. With its small size and blending colours the painting has, at first glance, a serene feel; however, what may have initially seemed like a lack of finish − the featureless face and disintegrating hands and feet − leaves a poignant and haunting impression on the viewer.

Seated Figure, 1997
Acrylic on paper
28 × 20 cm

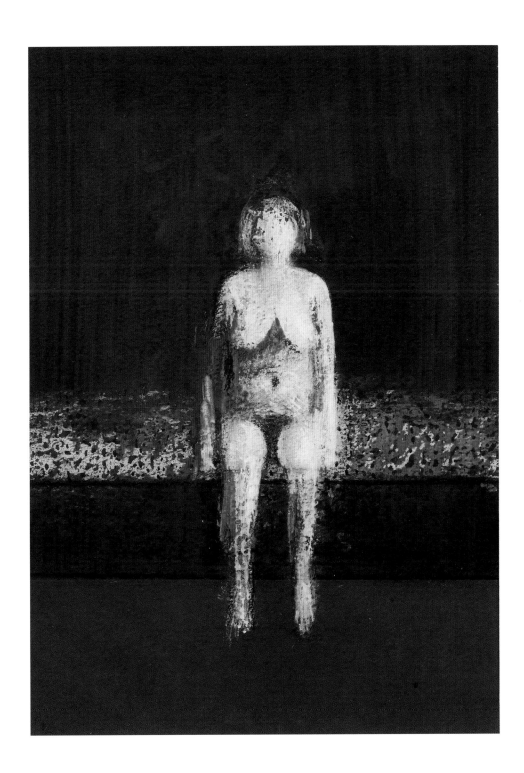

Maurice Cockrill RA

Born: 8 October 1936, Hartlepool, County Durham, UK
Elected RA: 15 November 1999
Category of Membership: Painter

Maurice Cockrill began painting at evening classes during the 1950s, before going on to study at Wrexham School of Art and the University of Reading (1960–4). Cockrill's first solo exhibition was held in London in 1984, and he has since exhibited extensively both in the UK and internationally, including retrospective exhibitions at the Walker Art Gallery, Liverpool (1995) and at the Royal West of England Academy, Bristol (1998). Among other prestigious awards Cockrill has received a British Council Award (1985) and been shortlisted for the Jerwood Prize (1994). He has earned significant acknowledgement for his role as both a teacher and poet, holding posts at Liverpool College of Art, Central St Martin's College of Art and Design, the Slade and the Royal College of Art. He was Keeper of the Royal Academy Schools from 2005 to 2011.

After moving to London in the early 1980s, Cockrill decided to break away from the Pop and photo-realist style of his earlier work and adopt the more romantic, expressionist style associated with his work today. He wanted a more direct, physical involvement with the paint, something that meticulous realism constrained. He now largely works standing up to allow bold painterly gestures, making strokes that are often over four feet, or pouring a thin, vertical rod of colour down the full length of the canvas.

This work makes clear how Cockrill builds up his paintings by layering and then cutting back. Yet he insists that his work is not abstract. 'Every picture is about something,' he says, 'even if I only find the title after I've finished.' There is indeed a striking energy to this work that is reflected in its hedonistic title. The stability of the rich red-and-green background sets the cut-away shapes free to dance before our eyes.

Dancing Around Midnight, 2012
Acrylic
200 × 249 cm

Peter Cook RA

Born: 22 October 1936, Southend-on-Sea, Essex, UK
Elected RA: 17 March 2003
Category of Membership: Architect

Peter Cook was a founding member of the visionary group Archigram. This avant-garde collective explored radical new possibilities for architecture, creating playful, Pop-inspired visions of a future heavily influenced by technology. The opening of the Kunsthaus in Graz in 2003, designed with Colin Fournier, marked the first physical manifestation of these concepts. In the intervening years Cook ran the Institute of Contemporary Arts (1969–71) and established and directed Art Net (1972–9). He was elected the Royal Academy's Professor of Architecture in 2005.

An overarching optimism pervades Cook's work and he has continued to expand the techniques and redefine the imagery of architectural drawings. For him, collaboration is pivotal to his creative methodology; architecture exists as a mutual flow of new ideas, each of which stems from a different source and cross fertilises with the next. In turn, these display themselves in drawings, writings and exhibitions as much as in buildings.

Cook's 'Comfo-Veg Club' is a project that builds on the same biological aesthetic that appears in his earlier work. It is a green space, amorphous and ambiguous, ever shifting in its spatial and material qualities. Designed for the SCI-Arc Gallery by Peter Cook and Gavin Robotham, *Towards Comfo-Veg* is a large-scale, site-specific installation; an experiential, vegetated world that invites visitors to sit and consider their surroundings. The same undulating forms and plant-like shapes dominate this print. This is the language of metamorphosis and hybridisation – a redefinition of traditional architectural imageries.

Comfo-Veg Club, 2008
Unique digital print from pen and watercolour
50 × 70 cm

COMFO-VEG CLUB   PETER COOK '2008

Eileen Cooper RA

Born: 10 June 1953, Glossop, Derbyshire, UK
Elected RA: 24 May 2001
Category of Membership: Printmaker

Eileen Cooper studied fine art at Goldsmiths College and the Royal College of Art, London. Solo exhibitions include Castlefield Art Gallery, Manchester (1986), Artsite, Bath (1987), Benjamin Rhodes Gallery, London (1988–97), Art First, London (1998–present), Dulwich Picture Gallery (2000) and three national public space tours. Paintings have been included in many exhibitions such as Hayward Annual, John Moores Liverpool, British Council international touring, Contemporary Arts Center, Cincinnati, USA, and 'Encounter: The Royal Academy in Asia'. Cooper was elected Keeper of the Royal Academy Schools in October 2011.

Figures are depicted with a linear vibrancy and a luminosity that is explosive in its liveliness, passion and tenderness. These are the very qualities that inform so much of her art, which at the same time reveals a strong academic training and continuous references to non-European cultures that serve to direct her work towards new and surprising discoveries.

In *Real Time* the two figures are entwined together as if dancing barefoot. Their gazes, however, seem curiously detached as if they are each absorbed in their own imaginary world. The existence of simultaneous but different realities is what Cooper often tries to capture in her work. Daydreams and fantasy intrigue her: 'Lots of people's lives are thrown together in my pictures, but there is also a strong sense of separateness. I find it fascinating that, in the busy lives that everyone leads, people have a sense of their own time, their own moments of reverie.'

Real Time, 2012
Oil on canvas
152 × 122 cm

Stephen Cox RA

Born: 16 September 1946, Bristol, UK
Elected RA: 9 December 2010
Category of Membership: Sculptor

Stephen Cox trained at the West of England College of Art, Bristol, Loughborough College of Art and the Central School of Art and Design, London. He had his first solo exhibition at Lisson Gallery, London (1976) and a major survey at Tate Britain (1986). He has shown extensively around the world and has been commissioned to produce many public sculptures, ranging from his large-scale works for Broadgate and the New Opera House, Cairo, in 1988 to a new altar for Canterbury Cathedral in 2005 and a holy water stoup in 2011. Notable awards include the Arts Council of Great Britain Award (1978, 1980), the Indian Triennale Gold Medal (1986) and the ACE Award for Art in a Religious Context (2007/8). His work is in the collections of Tate, the Victoria and Albert Museum and the British Museum.

Italian, Egyptian and Indian traditions are brought together in Cox's elegant, contemplative and often monumental sculptures, reflecting his strongly held conviction 'that what I do is part of the body of art in the world'. During the 1980s Cox lived in each of those countries, becoming acquainted not only with the sculptural canon but also the stone itself and ancient carving techniques handed down through generations. His practice in factories and studios in Italy, Egypt and India continues to concentrate largely on carving straight from stone, the emerging form being inspired as much by the nature of stone as Cox's awareness of cultural precedence. *Ladder Heads: Up* refers to the Tanmatras, the five elements of matter found in Samkhya cosmology. Each of the five pairs, or rungs, emphasises a different part of the face, which corresponds to a sense: the nose refers to smell and to earth; mouth is taste and water; eye to sight and fire; hand to touch and air; ear to hearing and ether. Arranged in a deliberate hierarchy, Cox has explored this concept before, and it is characteristic of how the artist's delicate and skilled carving brings narrative together with a formal sensitivity that resonates beyond its particular cultural context.

Ladder Heads: Up, 1993
Black Indian 'granite' with oil gel
164 × 80 × 10 cm

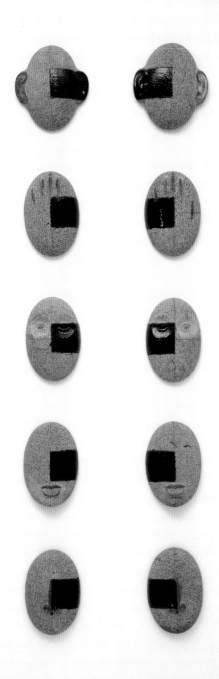

Tony Cragg RA

Born: 9 April 1949, Liverpool, UK
Elected RA: 23 May 1994
Category of Membership: Sculptor

Tony Cragg studied at Gloucestershire College of Art in Cheltenham. He went on to Wimbledon School of Art before attending the Royal College of Art, London. After graduating he moved to Wuppertal in Germany and began teaching at the Kunstakademie, Düsseldorf in 1978. In 2009 he became Director of the Kunstakademie, where he continues to teach.

Cragg has exhibited worldwide and his work is held in several public collections, including the Tate and Saatchi collections. Retrospective exhibitions have been held at the Tramway, Glasgow (1992) and the Whitechapel Gallery, London (1996). He has won several awards including the Turner Prize in 1988, the Piepenbrock Award for Sculpture in 2002 and the Praemium Imperiale Prize for Sculpture in 2007.

Minimalism and Concept Art are notable influences upon Cragg's body of work. His early sculptures were often made using found objects: industrial cast-offs, disposed household materials and raw matter. Later pieces focused on surface quality and the way in which this could be manipulated through the unexpected juxtapositions of material. Much of his work can be divided into two strands: Early forms (in which the container becomes a metaphor for the body) and Rational Beings; these are species of work to which he returns repeatedly.

It is, it isn't falls into the category of Rational Beings – a family of works characterised by tall columnar forms in bronze, wood, stone, plaster or steel. At some angles these are simply smooth, amorphous forms, at others the profile of a face emerges, only to disappear as you walk further around. Like the rest of the sculptures in this group (all of which bear a strong family resemblance) *It is, it isn't* was created by a complex process of building up elliptical cross-sections of steel on a vertical axis. This spiralling, dynamic form is representative of Cragg's intense curiosity about forms, materials, volume, line and surface.

It is, it isn't, 2011
Steel
Height 74 cm

Michael Craig-Martin RA

Born: 28 August 1941, Dublin, Ireland
Elected RA: 12 December 2006
Category of Membership: Painter

Born in Ireland and raised in Washington DC, Michael Craig-Martin studied at Yale School of Art before coming to Britain in 1966. He arrived with direct experience of American Pop Art and minimalism, and soon became one of the key figures in the first generation of British conceptual artists. His work is in most major public collections such as Museum of Modern Art, New York, the Centre Pompidou, Paris, and Tate. Recent major exhibitions include Kunsthaus Bregenz, Austria (2006) and a retrospective at the Irish Museum of Modern Art (2006–07).

Craig-Martin's neo-conceptualist theory that a work of art can be anything is embodied in his seminal work *Oak Tree* – a glass of water that he asserts is in fact an oak tree and which has been carried forth by the generation of Young British Artists who he had taught at Goldsmiths College, London, during the 1970s, '80s and early '90s.

Although Craig-Martin has maintained great conceptual clarity in his work, it is now characterised by the use of a broad and unexpected range of carefully outlined habitual objects or typography and rich, vibrant colour. *Untitled (Lock)* shows the elegance and restraint with which they are painted. A contemporary take on the still-life, his work has great visual integrity and a resonant rhythm that is found by initially using a computer to experiment with scale, juxtaposition and layering of images.

Boldly coloured and gently witty, Craig-Martin's paintings are so seductive that they might be described as eye-candy. Yet it is the combination of the immediate aesthetic appeal with the underlying concept that is of most interest. His work celebrates the fact that painting is about the moment, and can be simultaneously grand and modest. 'Painting is the only place where the physicality of the world is drawn into the mental world. It's where they meet.'

Untitled (Lock), 2012
Acrylic on aluminium
62 × 62 cm

Edward Cullinan RA

Born: 17 July 1931, London, UK
Elected ARA: 31 May 1989
Elected RA: 26 June 1991
Category of Membership: Architect

Edward Cullinan studied at Cambridge University and the Architectural Association. Upon graduating he joined the office of Denys Lasdun, after which he left to continue his studies at the University of California, Berkeley, in the early 1960s. He set up his own practice, Edward Cullinan Architects, in 1965. He has been awarded a number of accolades including a CBE in 1987 for Services to Architecture, the Royal Gold Medal in 2008 by the RIBA and in 2010 he was made a Royal Designer for Industry by the RSA.

Cullinan's work draws on the social ideals of modernism; community and the social patterns of modern institutions play an integral part. Unusual architectural components are often highlighted in bright colours or incongruous materials, such as the timber gridshell at the Weald and Downland Museum, West Sussex. Such imaginative detailing makes his projects both emotive and communicative. This more decorative aspect to his work does not prevent Cullinan's architecture from engaging with serious intellectual concerns. For example, when designing the maths faculty at the University of Cambridge he worked closely with its members, including Stephen Hawking, to ensure that the design provided the best possible environment for its users.

The exuberance that has come to characterise Cullinan's work is at play in this drawing. It combines an intimate understanding of the varied composition of London's streets with a suggestion of a narrative to create a bold and confident design. The drawing is both compelling and aesthetically appealing, communicating Cullinan's enthusiasm for the architecture that we see around us, and how it infuses and enriches our daily lives.

St Martin's Lane, 2012
Pen and ink on tracing paper
49.5 × 62.5 cm

Frederick Cuming RA

Born: 16 February 1930, London, UK
Elected ARA: 25 April 1969
Elected RA: 12 February 1974
Category of Membership: Painter

Frederick Cuming studied at Sidcup School of Art, and following two years of National Service he returned to four years' study at the Royal College of Art from 1951, gaining the Abbey Minor Scholarship. He has exhibited in both group and solo shows since 1953. In 2001 Cuming was the featured artist in the Royal Academy's 'Summer Exhibition' with a gallery dedicated to his work. His most recent exhibition was at the Brian Sinfield Gallery, Burford, in July 2012. He has received many awards including the Grand Prix Fine Art (Monaco, 1977), the Royal Academy's *House & Garden* Award and the Sir Brinsley Ford Prize (New English Art Club, 1986).

Cuming's work has a particularly impressionistic quality. His technique of layering colours quickly on canvas creates unique depictions of light and mood, which make his work distinctively recognisable. He says: 'I am not interested in pure representation; my work is about responses to the moods and atmospheres generated by landscape, still-life or interior. I am interested in the developments of twentieth-century painting, in abstraction, that has been present in all movements, and in new ideas and art forms. My philosophy is that the more I work the more I discover.'

This landscape of an East Sussex beach shows all the identifying Cuming traits, and his representation of a cloudy evening verges on the abstract. The juxtaposition of blue sky and dark cloud creates an engaging contrast.

Clouds Evening, Camber, 2011
Oil on board
110 × 110 cm

Gus Cummins RA

Born: 28 January 1943, London, UK
Elected RA: 27 May 1992
Category of Membership: Painter

Gus Cummins began what he considers an exploratory artistic journey at Sutton School of Art, progressing to Wimbledon School of Art and subsequently the Royal College of Art. He has taught at various art schools including the Chelsea School of Art, the Prince's Foundation and the Royal Academy Schools. He has exhibited at public and private galleries throughout the UK and in Norway, Holland, the United Arab Emirates and the USA. Among his many awards are first prize in the Hunting Group (1990, 1999) and the Jack Goldhill Sculpture Award at the Royal Academy of Arts in 2005.

Ambiguity is at the heart of Cummins' practice. He describes his process in humble, psychological terms: 'I try to create a parallel reality, to get an overview by standing a bit to one side – inviting the viewer to engage in speculation. I often feel unsure of what I'm working towards. It's an act of faith, accompanied by bouts of anxiety.' Therefore, when the work comes together there is some sense of catharsis: 'An extraordinary exhilaration creeps up – I'm aware that something is happening and I'm reassured that I am where I want to be.'

His abstract collage-like compositions also have a surreal nature: industrial dreamscapes that feel both monumental and dynamic. In this work the deconstructed elements tumble through space, transformed in his muted canvas into uncanny echoes of their practical selves.

Memories, 2008
Acrylic on canvas
150 × 200 cm

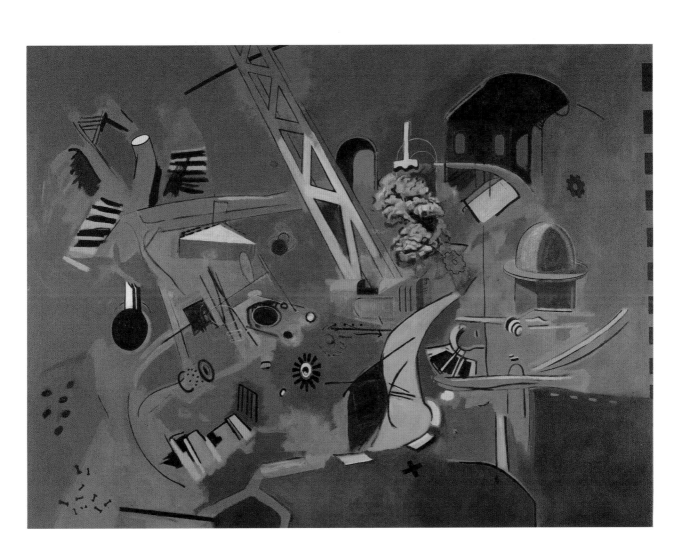

Trevor Dannatt RA

Born: 15 January 1920, London, UK
Elected ARA: 13 May 1977
Elected RA: 18 May 1983
Category of Membership: Architect

Trevor Dannatt has been categorised as working in the 'other tradition of modern architecture' as defined by his friend and fellow Academician, the late Sir Colin St John Wilson, with a fine respect for both the past and the future into which he sends his buildings. He studied at the Regent Street Polytechnic (now the University of Westminster), working in the famous practice of Maxwell Fry RA and Jane Drew. In 1948 he left to join the Royal Festival Hall design team under Sir Leslie Martin RA and his former tutor Peter Moro, which is notably the only permanent building constructed for the Festival of Britain. Strengthened by his involvement, Dannatt established his own practice a year after its completion in 1952. He feels indebted to a Welfare State that opened up educational opportunities to a wider social and economic spectrum. A rich dimension to his own career has been in teaching: he was formerly Professor of Architecture at the University of Manchester and later at the Royal Academy. He has also been closely involved in architectural publishing.

A sense of social usefulness also extends to the buildings he creates, paralleled by a school of Scandinavian architecture that foregrounds social value over formalism. Dannatt has been pleased to work on a host of social and educational buildings and in settings steeped with significance, including the combination room for Trinity Hall Cambridge, a new complex for the British Embassy in Riyadh, Saudi Arabia, and a major regeneration of the Royal Naval College buildings (Wren and Hawksmoor) for the University of Greenwich.

Yet Dannatt has a passionately aesthetic side. He started collecting paintings in 1944 and has collaborated with artists and designed gallery shows, most notably the Jackson Pollock exhibit at the Whitechapel Gallery in 1958.

Landscape Study, le petit champ Sark, CI, 1978
Pencil on cartridge paper
31 × 64 cm

Richard Deacon RA

Born: 15 August 1949, Bangor, Wales, UK
Elected RA: 21 May 1998
Category of Membership: Sculptor

Richard Deacon studied at Somerset College of Art, Taunton, and in London at St Martin's School of Art, the Royal College of Art and Chelsea School of Art. A string of national and international exhibitions followed, notably at the Riverside Studios (1984), Tate Britain (1985), the Whitechapel Gallery, London (1998) and Tate, Liverpool (1999). He has exhibited regularly at the Lisson Gallery, London, the Marian Goodman Gallery, New York, and the New Art Centre, Wiltshire. He won the Turner Prize in 1987 and in 1997 he was awarded the Chevalier des Arts et des Lettres, France.

Deacon has been a leading figure in British sculpture since the 1980s, when he began making a series of sheet-metal and laminated wood sculptures in simple organic shapes. Describing himself as a 'fabricator', Deacon has worked with a diverse range of vernacular materials, including polycarbonate, leather, cloth, glass and linoleum. He believes that making sculpture is akin to the way in which we use words as building blocks to create something new and lyrical. Raw materials that need to be carved or modelled are mostly rejected in favour of those whose essential form allows the structure of the finished sculpture to be self-evident. His work draws attention to the manufacturing process, as in this fine example where the rivets and welding joints are left exposed.

New Bases I is the first of a series of floor-based metal sculptures that explore the idea of mutually supportive structures. It resonates with one of Deacon's most celebrated works, *If The Shoe Fits*, 1981 (Tate collection). The aluminium exterior supports itself: there is no concealed armature and the interior negative space is as essential as the material elements. As with the artist's best work, it has controlled strength and integrity.

New Bases I, 2003
Aluminium
62 × 224 × 134 cm

Tacita Dean RA

Born: 12 November 1965, Canterbury, Kent, UK
Elected RA: 9 December 2008
Category of Membership: Painter

Tacita Dean graduated from Falmouth School of Art in 1988. She spent a year in Athens before taking her Higher Diploma at the Slade School of Fine Art between 1990 and 1992.

Dean is a visual artist who works primarily in film. In 1998 she was shortlisted for the Turner Prize and won the Hugo Boss Prize in 2006. In 2000 she received a DAAD Fellowship to spend a year in Berlin, and has lived there ever since. Her films are 16 mm and are often meditative depictions of places, people, objects, landscapes and seascapes. She has described film as 'the imprint of light on emulsion, the alchemy of circumstance and chemistry upon a support'. Her recent Turbine Hall installation *FILM* at Tate Modern championed the importance of keeping film as a medium in an increasingly digital age.

Dean also uses photography, drawing and found objects in her work, and since moving to Berlin has begun working in photogravure. *Dead Budgie Project* comes from a small envelope of photographs she found in the flea market documenting the death and burial of a woman's beloved pet. Fetishised and bizarre though the images are, they are nonetheless poignant and say much about human loneliness, attachment and the importance of ritual to grieving, albeit for a pet bird.

Dead Budgie Project, 2002
Set of 6 photogravures, printed on Hahnemühle Bütten 350 gsm paper (edition of 24)
no. 1 61 × 45 cm / no. 2 39 × 52 cm / no. 3 39.5 × 50.5 cm / no. 4 39.5 × 50.5 cm / no. 5 54 × 74 cm / no. 6 45 × 55 cm
Printed by Niels Borch Jensen and Mette Ulstrup, Copenhagen
Published by Niels Borch Jensen Galerie, Berlin

TACITA DEAN

DEAD BUDGIE PROJECT

BERLIN 1999

Anne Desmet RA

Born: 14 June 1964, Liverpool, UK
Elected RA: 26 May 2011
Category of Membership: Printmaker

A specialist printmaker, Anne Desmet has studied at both Oxford University's Ruskin School of Drawing and Fine Art and the Central School of Art and Design, London. In 1989 she was awarded a scholarship at the British School at Rome, and since 1991 has been a Fellow of the Royal Society of Painter-Printmakers. She has had numerous solo shows internationally: two significant retrospectives: 'Anne Desmet: Towers and Transformations' (Ashmolean Museum, Oxford, and touring, 1998–9) and 'Anne Desmet – Urban Evolution' (Whitworth Art Gallery, Manchester, and touring, 2009–10). Her work is held in many permanent public collections throughout the UK and the world. In addition to her skills as an artist, Desmet is an accomplished writer: she has had three books published on creative printmaking and is currently editor of *Printmaking Today* magazine.

Although Desmet works within a long tradition of printmaking techniques, including wood engraving and linocutting, she also draws, paints and prints more idiosyncratically and experimentally on a variety of materials to create innovative, textured and layered collages, which have achieved great acclaim. Her work varies in scale from small, detailed pieces to sweeping and more panoramic perspectives. Her linocut *Teatro Romano* falls within the former category, notable for the precision with which its architectural and geological subjects are rendered. Remarkable also is the sensitivity with which Desmet creates a feeling of harmony between the majesty of the built environment and the natural world, with its forbidding clouds and craggy rock formations. This unassuming print is a portal into classical Roman antiquity and, as with much of her work, it explores architectural landscapes and their evolution in terms of human aspiration and experience.

Teatro Romano, 2002
Two-block linocut
89 × 43 cm

Jennifer Dickson RA

Born: 17 September 1936, Piet Retief, South Africa
Elected ARA: 24 April 1970
Elected RA: 29 April 1976
Category of Membership: Engraver

Jennifer Dickson trained as a painter and printmaker at Goldsmiths College School of Art, London. Following further studies in Paris under S. W. Hayter, she taught at Brighton College of Art (now Brighton University) where she founded and directed the Graduate Printmaking Programme. Since her first solo exhibition in 1962 at the New Vision Centre, London, Dickson has exhibited extensively throughout the world, including in Canada, where she has lived since 1969. She was appointed a Member of the Order of Canada in 1995.

Dickson was one of the pioneers in the integration of photographic processes to printmaking. She has travelled extensively in Italy, France, Spain, Turkey and Britain documenting the historic landscape, and lecturing on the evolution of gardens. Her main pre-occupation as an artist is the survival of beauty over desecration.

Over a three-month period in 2005–06 an exhibition of Dickson's photographs titled 'Sanctuary: a Landscape of the Mind' was held in the Reynolds Room at the Royal Academy. Her exhibition 'The Last Silence' was circulated in Italy and Canada in the 1990s under the auspices of the Canadian Museum of Contemporary Photography, and is now in the permanent collection of the National Gallery of Canada.

In this print, which combines digital and manual techniques, we see Chiswick House, designed by Lord Burlington as his Salon of the Arts. Strongly influenced by the Italian architect Andrea Palladio, Burlington began the obsession with Palladian architecture in England in the eighteenth century, as suggested in this work's title. Burlington House, now home to the Royal Academy of Arts, was Lord Burlington's London seat. The artist chose to donate this image to 'RA Now' because of the link to Lord Burlington and the planned expansion of the Royal Academy into Burlington Gardens.

Lord Burlington Pays Homage to Palladio, 2011
Archival inkjet and watercolour print
64.5 × 75 cm

Philip Dowson PPRA

Born: 16 August 1924, Johannesburg, South Africa
Elected RA: 14 November 1985
President of the RA: 1993–99
Category of Membership: Architect

Philip Dowson studied architecture at Cambridge and the Architectural Association. He graduated in 1953 and then joined Ove Arup and Partners Structural Engineers. In 1963 he was a founding architect of Arup Associates, Architects and Engineers and became a senior partner of the Ove Arup Partnership in 1969. He was awarded a CBE in 1969 and was knighted in 1981, both for his services to architecture. In 1982 he was awarded the Royal Gold Medal for Architecture.

Throughout his career Dowson has celebrated architecture as a marriage between art and science. Rational, even scientific conditions of function, construction technique and the character of materials as the basis for design were fundamental in the firm's architectural approach, and Dowson's projects have long been known for their precision, lucidity, logic and elegance. These are traits that have frequently been applied to large and multifaceted buildings such as university departments and institutional headquarters. One innovation for which Dowson and his team are known is the concept of the 'tartan grid', a reworking of the classic modernist idea of a grid in which straight lines of varying widths and distances cross at right angles to create a dedicated zone of structure and services with the necessary flexibility.

In this depiction of Clare College Library, Dowson revisits the college at which he studied (1947–50) and explores the play of light with the rational, geometric mentality that is so prevalent in his work. This image was created in 1985, one year before the Forbes-Mellon Library designed by Dowson was completed. This celebration of the building echoes the way in which Arup Associates pioneered a way of working in historic contexts, seamlessly integrating the ancient and modern side by side.

Light Study. Entry of Clare College Library, Cambridge, 1985
Digital print (edition 2/30)
30.48 × 20.32 cm

Kenneth Draper RA

Born: 19 February 1944, Sheffield, Yorkshire, UK
Elected ARA: 30 May 1990
Elected RA: 26 June 1991
Category of Membership: Sculptor

Kenneth Draper, sculptor, draughtsman and painter, studied at Chesterfield College of Art and Kingston School of Art before attending the Sculpture Schools of the Royal College of Art. He has held teaching posts at Goldsmiths College School of Art and Camberwell School of Arts and Crafts. After winning the sculpture prize at 'Young Contemporaries' in 1965, he held his first solo exhibition at the Redfern Gallery, London, in 1969 and has received many significant commissions throughout his career. During the 1970s and '80s Draper was involved in numerous key exhibitions both in Britain and abroad, including 'British Sculptors '72' at the Royal Academy, the same year he received an important commission for the John Dalton Building, Manchester Polytechnic. In 1981 Warwick Arts Trust held a retrospective of his work, and Draper has since had exhibitions across Europe and North America.

As an artist working in both two and three-dimensional forms, he draws his energy and inspiration from the very ground that surrounds him, attracted, as he puts it, to the 'extreme universal energy of landscape which most acutely fires my imagination'. Living and working in Menorca, he is influenced by the mines, quarries and excavations, places that have felt the hand of man. These scars on the earth's surface are captured in the light of the sun and are rich with an 'overriding energy of colour' so wonderfully shown here in the burning, almost Rothko-red of this picture.

At the 2012 'Summer Exhibition' Draper was awarded the Hugh Casson Prize for Drawing for his work *Deep Quarry*, which is part of the same series of works as *Quarry – Ascension*, shown here.

Quarry – Ascension, 2009
Pastel on paper
56 × 56 cm

Buenos – Ascension '13

Bernard Dunstan RA

Born: 19 January 1920, Teddington, Middlesex, UK
Elected ARA: 24 April 1959
Elected RA: 9 July 1968
Category of Membership: Painter

Bernard Dunstan studied in London at the Byam Shaw School of Art and the Slade School of Fine Art. He followed this with a teaching career that began in 1946 and continued through to 1974, working at the West of England School of Art in Bristol, Camberwell School of Art, Byam Shaw School of Art, Ravensbourne Art College and City & Guilds of London Art School. Since 1952 he has held regular solo exhibitions at Roland, Browse and Delbanco, London, and later at Agnew's, London, and Stremmel Gallery in Nevada, USA. He was President of the Royal West of England Academy from 1979 to 1984 and has written several books, including *Learning to Paint* (1970) and *Painting Methods of the Impressionists* (1976).

'My motto is Ruskin's,' says Dunstan. 'Paint what you love and love what you paint.' For him this is most often intimate depictions of nudes and interiors with his wife, the painter Diana Armfield RA, or musicians. His paintings tend to be small in scale, in a style reminiscent of Vuillard and Sickert. Other influences are drawn from Renoir and Bonnard.

This scene shows an orchestra rehearsal, a subject Dunstan often revisited. The visibly quick brush strokes create instant movement in the image. The composition is cropped, giving a limited view of the scene, but the large music stand in the foreground makes the viewer feel part of the rehearsal – the conductor is pointing at an invisible member of the orchestra, but the engaging dynamic gives a sense that you might be next.

A Rehearsal, 2010
Oil on canvas
26.7 × 29.2 cm

Jennifer Durrant RA

Born: 17 June 1942, Brighton, Sussex, UK
Elected RA: 8 November 1994
Category of Membership: Painter

Jennifer Durrant's colourful, abstract work has an immediate charm that develops into resonant, discursive meanings upon deeper exploration. It is this gentle and gradual unfolding of her work that has garnered her a reputation as a meditative and spiritual artist. Durrant studied at Brighton College of Art (1959–66) and then at the Slade School of Art, London. In 1972 she travelled to the United States where she consolidated what had been a growing interest in the work of American Abstract Expressionists including Pollock, Gorky and Rothko In 1990 she showed in 'The Journey: A Search for the Role of Contemporary Art in Religious and Spiritual Life', during which one of her paintings was displayed in Lincoln Cathedral.

For Durrant, both creating a painting and experiencing it as the viewer are philosophical processes. She refers to the Hindu-Buddhist tradition of the mandala – a geometrically specific form of sacred art – suggesting that painting might fulfil a meditative and contemplative purpose.

In 2000 Durrant re-located to Italy, fuelled by a new love and a thirst for the kind of adventure only previously expressed on the canvas. This work is part of the *Uccelli* series (meaning birds in Italian) and was made in her rural Italian studio to the meditative sound of birdsong, which unconsciously became part of the painting: 'The two small collage series, *Uccelli* and *Last Conversations*, were made in a small space whilst waiting for my studio to be built, following my move to Italy and after a 30-year career of making stained, mural-sized canvases on the floor. For health reasons I now work on a smaller scale, often combining panels to make larger works.'

Durrant won the Athena Art Award in 1988, and with the prize money had planned on going to China to see the world-famous Buddhist caves covered in frescoes. However, she had to cancel the trip due to the Tiananmen Square massacre. This year she plans to finally make the journey.

From a Series, Uccelli, 2004
Acrylic on canvas on card, collage
17.5 × 11.5 cm

Tracey Emin RA

Born: 3 July 1963, Croydon, Surrey, UK
Elected RA: 27 March 2007
Category of Membership: Painter

Tracey Emin's first appearance at the Royal Academy was in the landmark 'Sensation' exhibition in 1997. Since then she has exhibited throughout the world. She has seduced and provoked in equal measure throughout her seminal career to date. Brittle and vulnerable, Emin has laid personal and raw emotions bare in her work, exploring taboo subjects, from her personal sexual history to abortion and rape. Although a household name, equally vilified and adored, and a darling of the YBAs (Young British Artists) and their elite circle, Emin has always foregrounded her start in life as a lost girl brought up in Margate in communicating the autobiographical identity that sits at the heart of her work.

Emin has a technical flexibility and can move with fresh enthusiasm between sculpture, photography, video, painting, drawing and installation. Indeed, her feminist and disruptive ideas are often conveyed through more traditionally 'feminine' mediums such as needlework.

In this example, the simplicity of the monoprint form underlines the unembellished naivety of the subject. Childlike handwriting suggests a life not long lived yet already regretful, somehow conflicting with the explicit, splayed pose of the female figure. That conflict between worldliness and fragility is what lends the work its poignancy and taps into a universal sense of vulnerability, whether acute or deeply buried.

A Fool, 2011
Monoprint
18.5 × 14.5 cm

I WAS A FOOL

MOST OF MY LIFE

A Fool   Tracey Emin 2011

Anthony Eyton RA

Born: 17 May 1923, Teddington, Middlesex, UK
Elected ARA: 30 April 1976
Elected RA: 20 November 1986
Category of Membership: Painter

Anthony Eyton studied fine art at Reading University in 1941 prior to serving in the army between 1942 and 1947. He resumed his studies at Camberwell School of Art, London (1947–50) and in 1951 received the Abbey Major Scholarship and as a result worked in Italy. In 1969 he was Head of Painting at St Lawrence College, Kingston, Ontario, and he has had a long teaching career at the Royal Academy Schools, from 1964 to 1999.

Eyton has exhibited extensively in a number of key group shows – namely at the Royal Academy, Tate and the Imperial War Museum. He is artist-in-residence at the Eden Project and has had solo shows in London at Browse & Darby and the Bankside Gallery, and in Austria at the Kunst Galerie, Salzburg. Eyton is a figurative painter and his travels through Asia, India and the continent have produced works that reflect the vitality and colour of each place. He is not simply a topological artist, but empathises with his location, reproducing visual rhythms through energetic brush strokes that keep the experience of the initial encounter alive.

In 2008 Eyton embarked on his first painting trip to Australia. During this period he created 35 oils and pastels of this 'ancient, powerful landscape', ranging from the people of Bondi Beach to the Sydney Opera House and Uluru. This painting of Hanging Rock is a departure from his better-known depictions of India and his garden in Brixton. It is energetically executed in a vibrant palette, reflecting a 'ferocity of light'. Each new painting is a fresh attempt to redress the balance of the use of the canvas as both a record of, and a metaphor for, the whims of nature.

Hanging Rock, 2008–09
Oil on canvas
150 × 150 cm

Stephen Farthing RA

Born: 16 September 1950, London, UK
Elected RA: 21 May 1998
Category of Membership: Painter

Stephen Farthing studied at London's St Martin's School of Art and the Royal College of Art, before spending a year at the British School in Rome. He has had an extensive teaching career and in 1990 was appointed Ruskin Master at the Ruskin School of Fine Art, which he directed for ten years. He currently holds the post of Rootstein Hopkins Research Professor of Drawing at the University of the Arts London. He has participated in many group exhibitions and represented Britain at the São Paolo Biennale in 1989, leading to further solo shows around the world. Farthing has been a regular participant in the John Moores Liverpool exhibitions, where between 1976 and 1999 he was a prize-winner on eight separate occasions.

Farthing's work as a painter sits midway between the conservative and the cutting-edge. His paintings are rich with references to a variety of disparate styles. 'I have dined with the devil in terms of becoming a modern artist,' he has said. 'I have taken hold of history, tried to understand it – and then used and abused it.'

Farthing's 'back story' paintings, of which *Black Bear #2* is a part, are a series of images painted with a text sometimes in reverse, sitting on the picture plane between the audience and the image. He weaves together a repeat image and a text in such a way that it prevents one being read independently of the other. The image of Black Bear, an Alaskan dice game, is both compromised and informed by the text. Farthing comments that his work is about purposefully degrading the initial image 'so it becomes not more ambiguous, but less what it was in the first place'.

Black Bear #2, 2010
Acrylic on cotton duck
102 × 76 cm

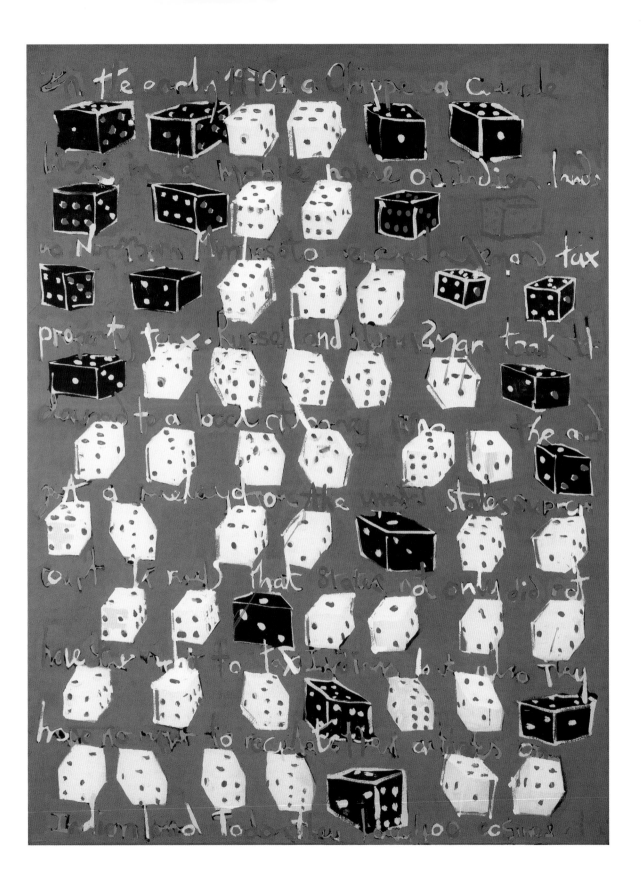

Norman Foster RA

Born: 1 June 1935, Manchester, UK
Elected ARA: 19 May 1983
Elected RA: 26 June 1991
Category of Membership: Architect

Norman Foster studied architecture at Manchester University before being awarded the Henry Fellowship to the Yale School of Architecture, where he was taught by Paul Rudolph. After returning to the UK in 1963 he set up the architectural practice Team 4 with Richard Rogers, who he had met at Yale, and in 1967 started to trade under his own name. Today, Foster + Partners is responsible for projects as varied as Wembley Stadium, the Hearst Tower in New York, the British Museum's Great Court and the transformation of the Reichstag in Berlin.

Completed in 2003, 30 St Mary Axe is an instantly recognisable part of London's skyline. It was London's first ecological tall building and is a radical design in many ways. The tower's radial plan breaks with the conventions of a traditional rectangular bloc, tapering towards its apex and widening in profile at its base allowing for a large public plaza. This distinctive form responds to the constraints of the site but also offers great improvements on the customary office model. The building appears more elegant and slender than a rectangular building of equivalent size; reflections are reduced and transparency is improved. Environmentally, its profile creates external pressure differentials that are exploited to drive a unique system of natural ventilation.

When receiving RIBA's Stirling Prize for his work on 30 St Mary Axe, Foster stated that the building can be seen as 'an embodiment of the core values that we have championed for more than 30 years: values about humanising the workplace, conserving energy, democratising the way people communicate within a building, and the way that building relates to the urban realm.' This unique model, a 3D print with a silver-plate finish, represents the building's triangulated structure, its most striking feature.

30 St Mary Axe: scale model, 2012
Black Perspex, ProtoGen resin, silver plating
38 × 15 × 15 cm

Peter Freeth RA

Born: 15 April 1938, Birmingham, UK
Elected ARA: 30 May 1990
Elected RA: 26 June 1991
Category of Membership: Engraver

Peter Freeth studied at the Slade School of Fine Art, London. In 1960 he won the Prix de Rome, which gave him the opportunity to live in Rome for three years and travel extensively throughout Italy. He has exhibited widely in mixed exhibitions in the UK, USA, Italy, Japan, India and Russia. Many public collections around the world hold his work including the British Museum, the Ashmolean Museum, Oxford, and the National Gallery, Washington DC. He was elected a Member of the Royal Society of Painter-Printmakers in 1991, and had a solo show in the Royal Academy's Tennant Room in 2008.

In 1971 Freeth received a postcard that was, in his own words, life-changing. It was four lines from his uncle, the printmaker Andrew Freeth RA, describing a new way of etching. Why he sent his nephew news about a technique that he wasn't interested in himself remains a mystery to Freeth. Nevertheless, this particular method has obsessed him ever since.

Although admitting that the process, which uses resin rather than traditional wax, is 'batty', he prefers it because it is a way of biting all the tones in one acid immersion, rather than consecutively. Despite its complexity it is able to manipulate infinite variations of grey. Freeth partly attributes his fascination with monochrome to the bleak wartime landscape of his Birmingham childhood, and also to Anthony Gross, his tutor at the Slade, who 'taught the gospel of black and white' and got Freeth into the habit of observational drawing. He is inspired by imagery that ranges from Old Master paintings to early films, poetry and hymns, memories and dreams, as well as the people whom he observes from his Muswell Hill studio. The masterful control of tone that Freeth achieves in this ethereal portrait reveals, however, that it is an all-consuming passion for etching that is the main driving force behind his art.

Doctor from St Lukes, 2004
Aquatint
49 × 60 cm

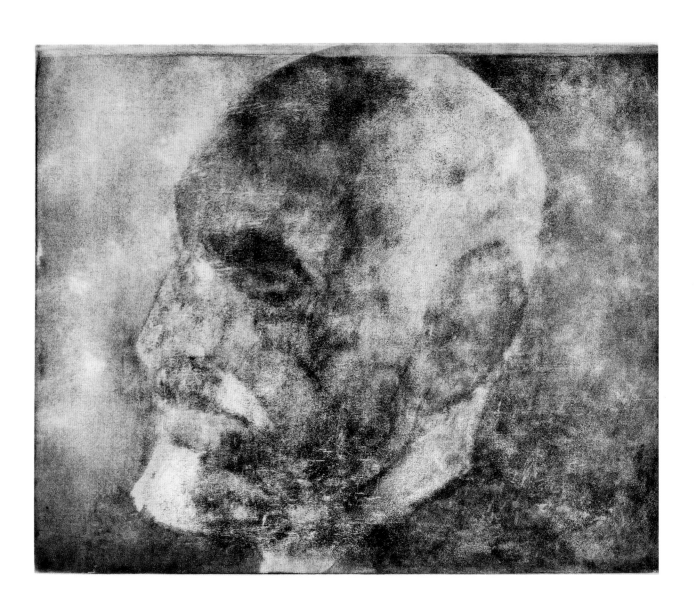

Frank O. Gehry Hon RA

Born: 28 February 1929, Toronto, Ontario, Canada
Elected Honorary RA: 21 May 1998

Raised in Toronto, Canada, Frank Gehry moved with his family to Los Angeles in 1947. He received his Bachelor of Architecture degree from the University of Southern California in 1954 and went on to City Planning at the Harvard University Graduate School of Design. He established his own his practice in Los Angeles in 1962 and has since designed and produced buildings across America, Europe and Asia, earning his reputation as one of the world's leading architects. He is perhaps most well known for the Guggenheim Museum in Bilbao, Spain, the Walt Disney Concert Hall in Los Angeles and the Dancing House in Prague. His buildings have received over 100 national and regional American Institute of Architects (AIA) awards, and he is the recipient of numerous prestigious international accolades, including the Pritzker Architecture Prize (1989), Companion to the Order of Canada (2003) and the Ordre National de La Legion d'Honneur, Republic Française (2005). Gehry's architectural drawings and models have been exhibited in major museums throughout the world.

The highly innovative, bold beauty of the geometric forms and materials in Gehry's designs challenge the modernist creed that form must follow function in favour of what he calls 'expression'. However, his buildings are not pure shape-making; he insists that his buildings address the culture and context of their sites, and that architecture is about relationships and should respond to the people that use them. He designed the museum to be accessible in both literal and metaphorical ways. The central hall has entry doors all around its circumference, while other parts of the campus face towards the museum: 'I was trying to make a building that had body language. People can come from all directions, and all kinds of people can come.' The project was not realised; nevertheless, this model shows how he skilfully manages to express the building's purpose within an aesthetically powerful design.

Museum Study, 2009
Basswood, vinyl, microply, acrylic
10.16 × 25.4 × 43.18 cm

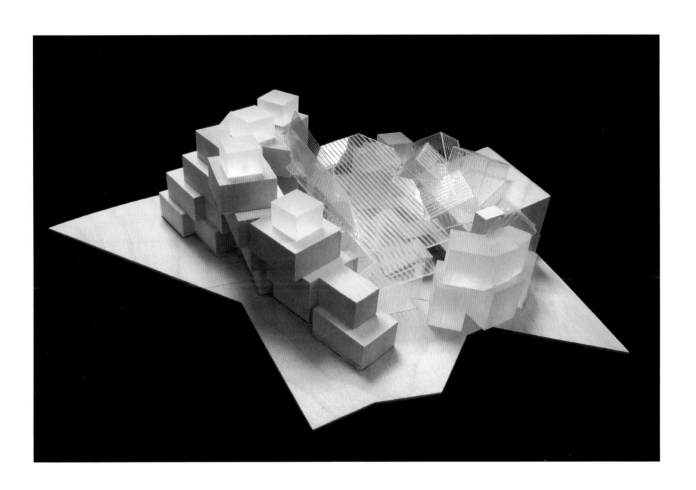

Antony Gormley RA

Born: 30 August 1950, London, UK
Elected RA: 23 May 2003
Category of Membership: Sculptor

Antony Gormley graduated from Trinity College, Cambridge, before getting an education of a rather less conventional kind during three years spent exploring India. On returning to London he completed creative studies at the Central School of Art and Design, Goldsmiths College and the Slade School of Art.

Gormley has exhibited throughout the world, with solo shows in London at the Whitechapel Gallery, the Serpentine Gallery and White Cube. He has also published several books, and won the Turner Prize in 1994. But it is his large-scale public artworks that have garnered him the greatest respect and placed him most permanently in Britain's collective imagination. His totemic sculpture *The Angel of the North* redefined sceptical popular attitudes towards sculpture, and has become as entrenched in Northern hearts as the 'hundreds and thousands of colliery workers' to whom Gormley wanted to 'bear witness'.

Yet despite the monumental, epoch-defining scope of much of his work, Gormley often sculpts from his own body – not to self-monumentalise, but rather to underline the universal, even self-effacing, basis of much of his work. Of his 100 cast iron sculptures on Crosby Beach in Sefton he said: 'It is no hero, no ideal, just the industrially reproduced body of a middle-aged man, trying to remain standing and trying to breathe...'

This sculptural installation from the *Ball Works Series,* as its playful title suggests, also speaks to the relationship between bodies, their function and the space they occupy. The figure is dynamic, animated somehow despite its stasis. But the component balls also evoke thoughts of cellular construction, our aggregate assemblage from a vast series of molecular balls: Gormley's work leads us to the realisation that our attraction to other bodies is only matched by the imperceptible attraction within our own.

Standing Matter XXXIV, 2011
Cast iron
Height 192 cm

Piers Gough RA

Born: 24 April 1946, Brighton, Sussex, UK
Elected RA: 5 December 2001
Category of Membership: Architect

Piers Gough, a graduate of the Architectural Association, is an architect known for his humility and creative playfulness. Always true to principles laid down during formative years spent with Peter Cook and the Archigram Group, Gough founded his firm – Campbell Zogolovitch Wilkinson and Gough – in 1975. Alongside commercial work he has enjoyed great success in creative projects: he designed the RA's exhibition on Sir John Soane in 1999 and the hugely popular show on Sir Edwin Lutyens at the Hayward Gallery in 1981, while his Green Bridge transformed a pocket of East London. His work also met with acclaim during the early redevelopment of the London Docklands.

This ebullient drawing is typical of Gough's comfort designing within the context of the urban environment. When he designed his friend Janet Street Porter's London end-of-terrace house, he played with conventions of London architecture and inventively incorporated found materials. Similarly, here he demonstrates boldness in his vision that feels optimistically experimental, particularly considering that these undulating towers were designed to serve the practical purpose of student accommodation next to the Emirates Stadium.

Gough has worked on similarly functional buildings to provide housing across North London and the rest of the city, and expresses an interest in the social life of architecture. It is also fitting that these buildings of his are used and inhabited by the general public – as a student it was Pop Art's conscious interaction with ordinary people that Gough found most inspiring. And he sees himself on a less elevated plane than many of his contemporaries. A plucky Tribal Tower sparring with its vast stadium neighbour perhaps says something about Gough's understanding of his own position within a landscape of fellow architects.

Tribal Towers, 2012
Pencil on paper mounted on aluminium
51 × 76 cm

TRIBAL TOWERS STUDENT HOUSING AT THE EMIRATES · CZWG ARCHITECTS

Anthony Green RA

Born: 30 September 1939, Luton, Bedfordshire, UK
Elected ARA: 23 April 1971
Elected RA: 1 March 1977
Category of Membership: Painter

Born in London, Anthony Green exhibited in 'Young Contemporaries' in 1956, the year he began studying at the Slade School of Art. After graduating in 1960 he received a French Government scholarship to travel and study in Paris for a year. Two years later he held his first one-man show at the Rowan Gallery, London, and he has since exhibited and taught extensively both in Britain and abroad. He received a Harkness Fellowship to the United States in 1967 and his first major retrospective was at the Royal Academy in 1978. He was shortlisted for the Jerwood Painting Prize in 1996, and in 2008 a retrospective of his work was held at Richmond Hill Gallery.

Throughout his career Green has developed his own personalised perspective, akin to a fish-eye lens, that affords his work an instantly recognisable and quirky charm. His paintings break free of the formal shapes and constraints of a traditional approach, favouring oddly shaped supports and, more recently, freestanding structures. Inspired by his immediate surroundings, Green's work from the 1960s onwards creates 'a continuing chronicle of the artist's life and immediate family', in particular his relationship with his beloved wife, Mary, who he met while studying at the Slade. With his wonderfully rich and vivid palette, these tender and personal scenes are both captivating and beautifully poignant. In this painting the pair are seen almost as one, inextricably intertwined on the bed that forms the central focus, around which the rest of the composition orientates like petals opening from the centre of a flower.

Paradise 1, 1988
Oil on board
221 × 228.6 cm

Spencer de Grey RA

Born: 7 June 1944, Farnham, Surrey, UK
Elected RA: 9 December 2008
Category of Membership: Architect

Spencer de Grey studied architecture at Cambridge University under Sir Leslie Martin. He is now a senior partner and joint Head of Design at Foster & Partners, which he joined in 1973. De Grey has overseen a wide range of acclaimed projects both in the UK and abroad, including the Sackler Galleries at the Royal Academy, nine new City Academy schools, the Great Court at the British Museum, HM Treasury in Whitehall, the redevelopment of Dresden Station, Germany and Boston Museum of Fine Arts, USA; he has recently won a competition to rework the New York Public Library. He is Chairman of both the Building Centre Trust and the Cambridge University School of Architecture Advisory Board. He was awarded a CBE in 1997.

This silver-plated 3D print is a unique model of the Sage Gateshead, the £70m performing arts centre on the banks of the Tyne that was completed under de Grey's direction in 2004. Its sleek, billowing roof envelops a complex that is both a regional music centre of international standing and a much-loved social space. Acoustic excellence was at the heart of the project, with de Grey and his team travelling through Europe in pursuit of the best auditory experience. Home of the Northern Sinfonia, the Sage encompasses three structurally separate concert halls, the largest of which is modelled on the renowned acoustics of the Musikvereinsaal, Vienna. Its interiors are largely ash and birch, which create a rich and reverberant sound, while suspended over the stage are panels of fibreboard and plywood that are able to move high above the stage in order to adjust to different musical needs. The concourse itself has become a venue for informal music-making and education. The Sage's strikingly beautiful, sensitively designed glass and stainless steel shell nurtures and enhances all facets of music and performance.

The Sage Gateshead: scale model, 2012
Black Perspex, ProtoGen resin, silver plating
22.6 × 20.3 × 85 cm

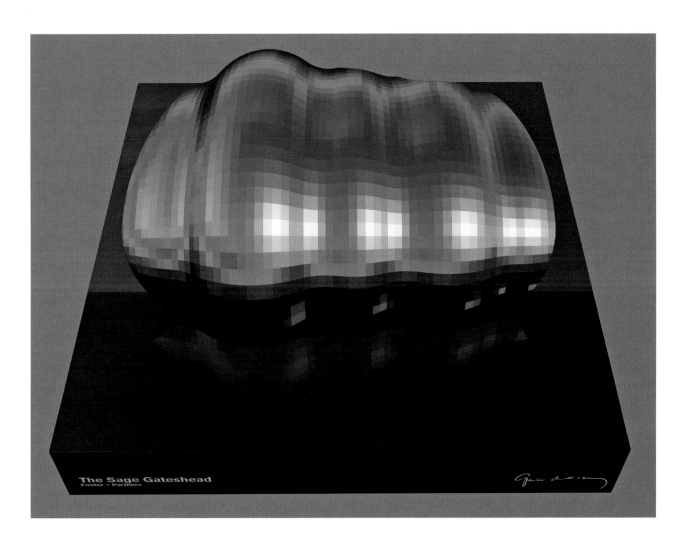

The Sage Gateshead
Foster + Partners

Nicholas Grimshaw PPRA

Born: 9 October 1939, Hove, Sussex, UK
Elected RA: 23 May 1994
President of the RA: 2004–11
Category of Membership: Architect

Sir Nicholas Grimshaw was educated at the Edinburgh College of Art before being awarded a scholarship to the Architectural Association School of Architecture, where he graduated with honours in 1965. He immediately started his own practice and won many architectural awards in the 1960s and '70s for buildings notable for their innovative approach to construction and detailing.

Today, his practice – Grimshaw – operates internationally with offices in London, New York, Sydney and Melbourne. Grimshaw is best known for projects as diverse as Waterloo International Station, phase II of the ExCeL Exhibition Centre, the Cutty Sark Conservation Project, the RAC Regional Headquarters in Bristol, Sainsbury's urban quarter in Camden, London, the Frankfurt Trade Fair Hall, and Southern Cross Station in Australia, which earned him the RIBA's Lubetkin Prize in 2007.

These two models represent the minimal yet striking organic structure of what is perhaps Grimshaw's most innovative and singular design: the Eden Project in Cornwall, completed in 2000. The complex is dominated by two vast enclosures that house a spectacular variety of plant species, each enclosure emulating a natural biome. The biomes, threaded around the 2.2 hectare site, are formed of a sequence of two sets of four inter-linked geodesic transparent domes, the largest encapsulating a humid tropical environment, the other a warm temperate Mediterranean environment. The Eden Project's biomes are designed to mimic these alien climates using minimal additional energy: most of the heat is generated passively by storing the sun's energy within the biomes and in the rock of the site. The continuing success and popularity of this remarkable building is a testament to Grimshaw's reputation as one of Britain's most gifted architects.

Eden Project Biomes, 2002
Rapid prototype model with a metallic finish
Large biome 14 × 24 × 14 cm
Small biome 9 × 18 × 9 cm

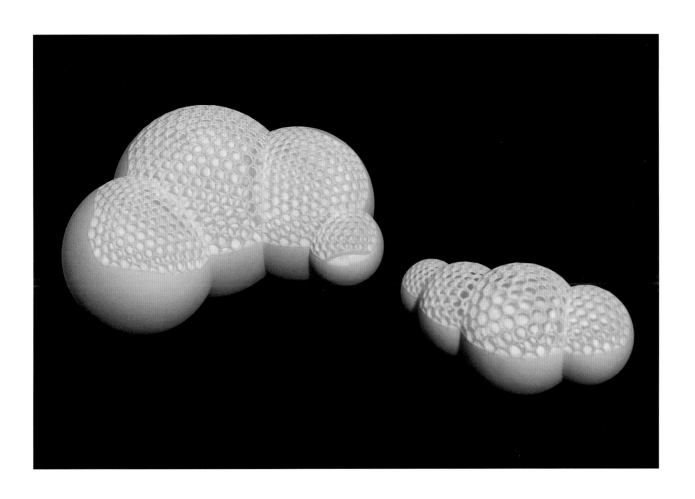

Zaha Hadid RA

Born: 31 October 1950, Baghdad, Iraq
Elected RA: 25 May 2005
Category of Membership: Architect

Zaha Hadid is arguably the greatest architect Iraq has ever produced, her talent leading her to break boundaries and expectations. This was underlined in 2004 when she was the first woman to win the highly prestigious Pritzker Architecture Prize.

Born in Baghdad, she studied Mathematics at the American University of Beirut, developing a sense of mathematical precision that is evident in her work. She then moved to London to study at the Architectural Association under Rem Koolhaas and Elia Zenghelis, who subsequently became her employers at the Office for Metropolitan Architecture. Koolhaas held her in high esteem, calling her 'a planet in her own inimitable orbit'. She was made partner in 1977 and just two years later established her own practice.

An appreciation of the transformative power of good teaching remained with her, and she has taught at institutions the world over, including Eero Saarinen Visiting Professor of Architectural Design at the Yale School of Architecture and her current role as Professor at the University of Applied Arts Vienna, Austria. She has won a consistent stream of challenging architectural competitions and has been awarded exclusive commissions throughout the world, from Weil am Rhein to Guangzhou.

Visionary and distinctive, Hadid's buildings are known for their seductive, curved lines and sense of fluidity both in form and situation. These hallmarks are evident in this photograph by Hélène Binet of Hadid's auditorium in Azerbaijan. The image conveys the bold scale of Hadid's design, but more unusually, the print also captures the moment of a building mid-construction in which it appears magically woven into its environment; an otherworldly apparition but with a definite sense of belonging. This is what sets Hadid apart as an architect: her unfettered imagination together with an expert command of mathematics allow her to bring the most creative and surprising buildings to life.

Auditorium Entrance, Heydar Aliyev Centre, Baku, 2007–12
Digital black-and-white silver gelatin print (edition of 6, plus 2 artist's proofs); photograph by Hélène Binet
44.5 × 56.5 cm

Nigel Hall RA

Born: 30 August 1943, Bristol, UK
Elected RA: 17 March 2003
Category of Membership: Sculptor

Nigel Hall studied sculpture at the Royal College of Art, London, where he later became a tutor. After graduating he spent two years in the United States on a Harkness Fellowship. He was Head of MA Sculpture at Chelsea School of Art and a faculty member of the British School in Rome. He is well represented in numerous public collections including Tate, The Museum of Modern Art, New York, the National Gallery of Australia, Canberra, Nationalgalerie, Berlin and the Tokyo Metropolitan Museum of Art, among many others. Hall has also undertaken both private and public large-scale, site-specific commissions internationally. In 2008 he had a solo survey show at the Yorkshire Sculpture Park, Wakefield.

Hall's love of sculpture stems from early childhood as his grandfather was a West Country stonemason. The cutting of stone informed his later preoccupation with sculpture and drawing. He now sculpts in a variety of materials, producing work that ranges in size from the intimate to the grand scale. He also makes large, lyrical charcoal and gouache drawings in which saturated pigments give weight to precise, geometric linear forms. Hall considers his graphic work to be entirely separate to his sculptures, insisting that they are not merely preparatory sketches; they too are preoccupied with implied volume and space. This is suggested through form, light and shadow, inspired by landscape and music. 'My work has always been about place. I am fascinated by the way geometry can be discerned in landscape.'

The looping curves and balance of colour and tone in *Drawing 1553* leads the eye on a particular journey, and manifestly depicts his interest in the way 'the landscape often slips away into a pure, empty space, so you get a sense of the eye moving in a circle between foreground and background, then back to the brain'.

Drawing 1553, 2010
Gouache and charcoal on paper
61 × 153 cm

David Hockney RA

Born: 9 July 1937, Bradford, Yorkshire, UK
Elected RA: 26 June 1991
Category of Membership: Painter

David Hockney studied at Bradford School of Art and then the Royal College of Art, London (1959–62) where he was awarded the Royal College of Art gold medal in 1962 in recognition of his mastery as a draughtsman and his innovative paintings. His work was featured in the 1961 exhibition 'Young Contemporaries', which heralded the birth of British Pop Art. He settled Los Angeles in the early 1960s and is still closely associated with California and the large body of work he produced there over many decades. Hockney was commissioned in 1972 to design sets and costumes for Stravinsky's opera *The Rake's Progress* at Glyndebourne. Other opera design commissions followed, most notably at the Metropolitan Opera in New York.

Many of the world's prestigious galleries and museums have work by Hockney in their contemporary collections. He has exhibited internationally over his long career, and in January 2012 the Royal Academy of Arts held a major exhibition 'David Hockney RA: A Bigger Picture', which featured recent paintings, ipad drawings and film work focusing on landscape, primarily that of East Yorkshire. The exhibition then toured to the Guggenheim in Bilbao, and the final stage opens at Museum Ludwig, Cologne, in October 2012. Always exploring new forms of visual expression and often employing technology in the process, printmaking – and the possibilities it affords – has played a major part in Hockney's artistic output. This work from 2008 is drawn on the computer to be printed. 'There are advantages and disadvantages to anything new in mediums for artists, but the speed allowed here with colour *is* something new.' The skill Hockney demonstrates here in his draftsmanship and employment of colour gives this computer drawing all of the qualities of his oils and watercolours.

In January 2012 Hockney was appointed a member of the Order of Merit by The Queen.

Autumn Leaves, 2008
Inkjet printed computer drawing on paper (edition 23/25)
88.9 × 118.1 cm

Michael Hopkins RA

Born: 7 May 1935, Poole, Dorset, UK
Elected RA: 28 May 1992
Category of Membership: Architect

An alumnus of the Architectural Association, Sir Michael Hopkins founded Hopkins Architects with his wife, Patty, in 1976. He was one of the early champions of British 'high-tech' architecture and has continued to be at the forefront of innovative, sustainable and energy-efficient design internationally. He has been knighted for Services to Architecture and has been awarded a CBE and the RIBA Gold Medal for Architecture (1994). He is a past President of the Architectural Association and has served as a trustee of the British Museum.

The first of four permanent Olympic venues to be completed, the Velodrome was unveiled on 13 January 2011 ahead of time and to budget and was greeted with much critical acclaim. Guided by the practice's ethos of placing architectural, environmental and social convictions at the heart of any project, Hopkins Architects' design took inspiration from the simplicity and efficiency of the bicycle itself. Performance and practicality were priorities, and in both it has excelled. By meticulously tailoring the track geometry and perfecting the temperature and environmental conditions within the venue, it is the fastest velodrome that exists, and has been unanimously praised by professional cyclists. It is also the most sustainable of the Olympic venues. Openings in the external timber cladding allow air to flow freely through the building while its compact design and use of significant natural daylight keeps energy requirements low. Its simplicity and efficiency has created a strikingly neat and elegant building, with its lightweight double-curving cable net structure and distinctive sustainable western red cedar-clad upper bowl reflecting the geometry and dynamism of the steeply banked track itself.

As this photograph shows, functional excellence has been achieved without forgoing aesthetic integrity: the Velodrome's lean and graceful form is a stylish addition to the London skyline.

London 2012 Velodrome, 2012
Digital photograph by Andrew Unterhalter
27 × 120 cm

Ken Howard RA

Born: 26 December 1932, London, UK
Elected ARA: 19 May 1983
Elected RA: 26 June 1991
Category of Membership: Painter

Ken Howard was born in London and studied at Hornsey School of Art. After completing National Service with the Royal Marines he returned to study at the Royal College of Art, winning a British Council Scholarship to study in Florence in his final year. He exhibited at the Plymouth Art Centre in 1955, and has since gone on to hold numerous solo exhibitions throughout Britain and abroad, in particular with the New Grafton Galleries from the 1970s, and since 2002 with Richard Green, London. He has won many prizes and commissions throughout his career, and in 1973 and 1979 the Imperial War Museum appointed him official artist in Northern Ireland.

With his careful and considered orchestration of tone and colour, Howard uses light as the primary tool in much of his work, whether in his tranquil Venetian scenes or his highly popular studio studies, both of nudes and still-lifes. Nigel Billen wrote that Howard paints 'like all great artists, for the moment', and finds a freshness in the everyday that he transplants so masterfully to the canvas in his instantly recognisable visual language. He captures and reveals the inherent beauty of even the most inanimate objects, as can be seen in this painting, with the light caught and reflected off the silverware and a warmth of palette typical of his output.

Bitta's Silver, c. 2008
Oil on canvas
50.8 × 61 cm

Gary Hume RA

Born: 9 May 1962, Kent, UK
Elected RA: 24 May 2001
Category of Membership: Painter

Gary Hume graduated from Goldsmiths College, London, in 1988. Following his first solo show at Karsten Schubert, London, in 1989 he rapidly established an international reputation, exhibiting in numerous significant group exhibitions throughout the 1990s. He was shortlisted for the Turner Prize in 1996 and won the Jerwood Painting Prize in 1997.

Hume claims that he is an artist without ideas, and hates stories in paintings. He says that a piece of his work begins with trips to second-hand bookshops to buy material on whatever interests him at the time. He can, he says, immediately tell if he can use an image. He will trace that image onto acetate with a marker pen, and then project it onto the wall where he traces the lines onto the surface of the painting. In 1993 Hume abandoned the iconic *Doors* series that had initially brought him to prominence and began to

choose flora, fauna and portraiture as his subjects.

Although Hume refers to himself as a 'beauty terrorist', preferring to leave the picture enigmatic and inexplicable, he does not create throwaway images. The flat, simply coloured representation of flowers in *Untitled* renders them defiantly solid and unnaturalistic. They are a moment stilled, created from a 'wonderful solitary experience', and so a certain amount of time is required for the viewer to feel truly absorbed in the image. Hume believes that 'art is not about absolute concrete affirmations. Art has questions and doubts and ups and downs of preference.' He has often expressed a desire to give 'leaden boots' to gallery visitors viewing his paintings so that they might spend more time in front of them: 'That's because *I* spend so much time looking at them. I can look at them a long, long time without getting bored. I disappear.'

Untitled, 2008/2011
Charcoal on paper, UV Perspex and gloss paint
130 × 90.5 cm

Paul Huxley RA

Born: 12 May 1938, London, UK
Elected ARA: 27 May 1987
Elected RA: 26 June 1991
Category of Membership: Painter

Paul Huxley went to Harrow School of Art at the age of 13. In 1956 he was accepted to the Royal Academy Schools, graduating in 1960. He taught at the Royal College of Art, London, from 1976, where he was made Professor of Painting in 1986 and Honorary Fellow and Professor Emeritus in 1998. He obtained first prize in the Eastern Arts Exhibition (1983) and a National Art Collections award for Outstanding Service to the Arts (1995). He was a member of the advisory panels for the Arts Council and the Serpentine Gallery, a Trustee of Tate, and is currently Treasurer of the Royal Academy of Arts.

Huxley has made abstract paintings over his 60-year career, preferring to invent an alternative world governed by its own laws. A Harkness Fellowship to New York in the early 1960s proved particularly formative for the young artist as it brought him into contact with leading American Abstract Expressionists. His visit culminated in a solo exhibition where he first developed the divided canvases that are now so characteristic of his work.

Over the last decade Huxley has made a series of paintings on a Chinese theme, and he had recent exhibitions in Seoul, Beijing and Singapore. He sees a parallel between the shapes he paints and the bold characters found in Chinese signage – both interplay between abstract form and language.

In July 2011 Huxley was invited by the two painters Qu Yan and Ying Sheng Yang to join a group of artists in Xu Cun Village, in the mountainous region of Shanxi Province to the south-west of Beijing. Huxley completed three paintings in the three weeks of his stay; *The Link* developed out of the series he began there.

The Link, 2012
Acrylic on canvas
137 × 137 cm

Timothy Hyman RA

Born: 17 April 1946, Hove, Sussex, UK
Elected RA: 26 May 2011
Category of Membership: Painter

Timothy Hyman studied at the Slade School of Fine Art. He has exhibited widely in the UK, Italy and India and he won the National Portrait Gallery Travel Award in 2007. As well as being a figurative painter, Hyman is also a writer, lecturer and curator. He has published monographs on Sienese painting and the work of Pierre Bonnard, and has also curated exhibitions at Tate, the Institute of Contemporary Arts and Hayward Gallery.

Hyman is probably best known for his narrative renditions of London. Influenced by such artists as Brueghel, Lorenzetti, Beckmann and Bonnard, he explores his personal relationship, both real and mythologised, with the city in which he lives and works. His pieces are often characterised by his use of vivid colours, shifting scales and distorted perspectives.

London is once again the setting of this painting. It is a surprising rediscovery of Hyman's well-known surroundings. It gives the sense, as one critic has commented about another of his works, 'similar to that of the astronaut contemplating the blue planet from outer space'. At the centre of this familiar, yet alien world, are the recognisable figures of Hyman himself and his wife Judith. As the painting's title suggests, the overarching metaphor in this piece is that of the individual life journey. As he and his wife embrace at the centre of the picture, elements of Hyman's personal iconography rush around them in a whirl of colour.

'His aim is always to switch the self into some realm beyond it,' writes David Gervais; his painting 'may be violently self-revealing but it is not confessional: the emotion actually refers to something as complex and communal as London, the personal in the impersonal'.

Turning my Own Wheel, 2002
Oil on canvas
162 × 130 cm

Albert Irvin RA

Born: 21 August 1922, London, UK
Elected RA: 10 December 1998
Category of Membership: Painter

Born in London, Albert Irvin studied at Northampton School of Art, and after five years' of service in the RAF during the Second World War he went on to study at Goldsmiths College, London. He has held teaching posts throughout Britain, most notably at Goldsmiths (1962–83), and in 1968 he won a Travel Award to America from the Arts Council. His first solo exhibition was held in 1960 at 57 Gallery, Edinburgh, and his first major retrospective was at the Serpentine Gallery, London, in 1990.

Inspired by American abstract art of the 1950s, Irvin maintains and develops an impressive abstract visual language that has remained characteristically bold throughout his career. With confident sweeping strokes in striking and vivid colours, he captures the energy and excitement with which he paints, and imbues his work with this sense of passion and immediacy.

Harmony is an impressive example of the artist's more recent output; the eye of the viewer is drawn across the expanse of canvas, with the woven, multicoloured brush strokes set against a rich tangerine background. One is able to sense the freedom and free-flowing familiarity with which he handles his paint, with a joy and a palette that is so clearly Irvin's own.

Harmony, 2009
Acrylic on canvas
183 × 153 cm

Bill Jacklin RA

Born: 1 January 1943, London, UK
Elected ARA: 1 June 1989
Elected RA: 26 June 1991
Category of Membership: Painter

Bill Jacklin initially studied graphic design for a year at Walthamstow School of Art, London, before returning there to study painting in 1962. In 1967 he gained an MA from the Royal College of Art, London. His first solo show was at Nigel Greenwood Gallery, and since the 1970s he has exhibited regularly with Marlborough Gallery in London and New York. His work is in the collections of Yale Center for British Art, New Haven, Connecticut, Victoria and Albert Museum, London, and The Metropolitan Museum of Art, New York, among many others. He has lived and worked in New York since 1985.

Jacklin only anticipated a year away from England, but he found the move to New York invigorating and it re-ignited his imagination. He felt an urge to document the energy and the people of his new city, and thus began his lifelong chronicle of New York life seen through the eyes of an outsider. Grand Central Station is a favoured subject of Jacklin's, and he captures the fleeting figures passing through the iconic, cathedral-like building with characteristically fluid brush strokes. With sunlight streaming past the prominent US flag, he conjures the optimism and energy of a morning in the city. Yet it could be a moment from any point over the last century – time somehow seems to be split. Although the building, light and flag speak reassuringly of constancy, there is a great sense of motion and temporality. The station is a benign host to an ever-changing crowd. As with much of Jacklin's work, *Lucky Strike, Grand Central V* serves as an existential reminder that the time we have on earth is brief. Like the commuters in the painting, we are part of a relentless cycle of change.

Lucky Strike, Grand Central V, 2008
Oil on canvas
76 × 102 cm

Tess Jaray RA

Born: 31 December 1937, Vienna, Austria
Elected RA: 16 March 2010
Category of Membership: Painter

Tess Jaray studied in London at St Martin's School of Art and the Slade School of Art, where she later became its first female teacher. Solo exhibitions include the Whitechapel Gallery (1973), the Ashmolean Museum, Oxford, Whitworth Art Gallery, Manchester, and the Serpentine Gallery, London. Her work features in many public collections, including Tate and the British Museum, and her paving designs can be seen in Centenary Square, Birmingham, and the forecourt of London's Victoria Station. In 2012 the Royal Academy re-published a book of her collected writings, *Painting: Mysteries and Confessions* and published her artist's book, *Thresholds*.

Throughout her career Jaray has kept faith with a formal language that is both constant and infinitely renewable. Light and geometry are her vocabulary, which she expertly employs to investigate the effects that pattern, repetition and colour have on our perceptions. Her work is formal and precise; groups of shapes are arranged on plain backgrounds and paint is applied absolutely flat. She is scrupulously self-disciplined in her work, rejecting all but the essential. 'Nothing must be redundant. The eye should not be able to rest on any one area of the painting without being drawn, as if magnetically, to another part, and yet another, and eventually to the original area, to move on once again. This way there is no final resolution and the painting remains constantly active.'

Jaray is acutely aware of the vitality inherent within rhythm and pattern, and harnesses this so that the paintings are ultimately expressive and personal. As she explains, they are 'to do with a need to use my experience, somehow to make manifest part of what I have felt and feel about life, so that experience is not lost, but can be brought to life again, relieved through metaphor and the act of painting itself'.

Field, Brown with Five Lines, 2011
Cut-out on panel
80 × 122 cm

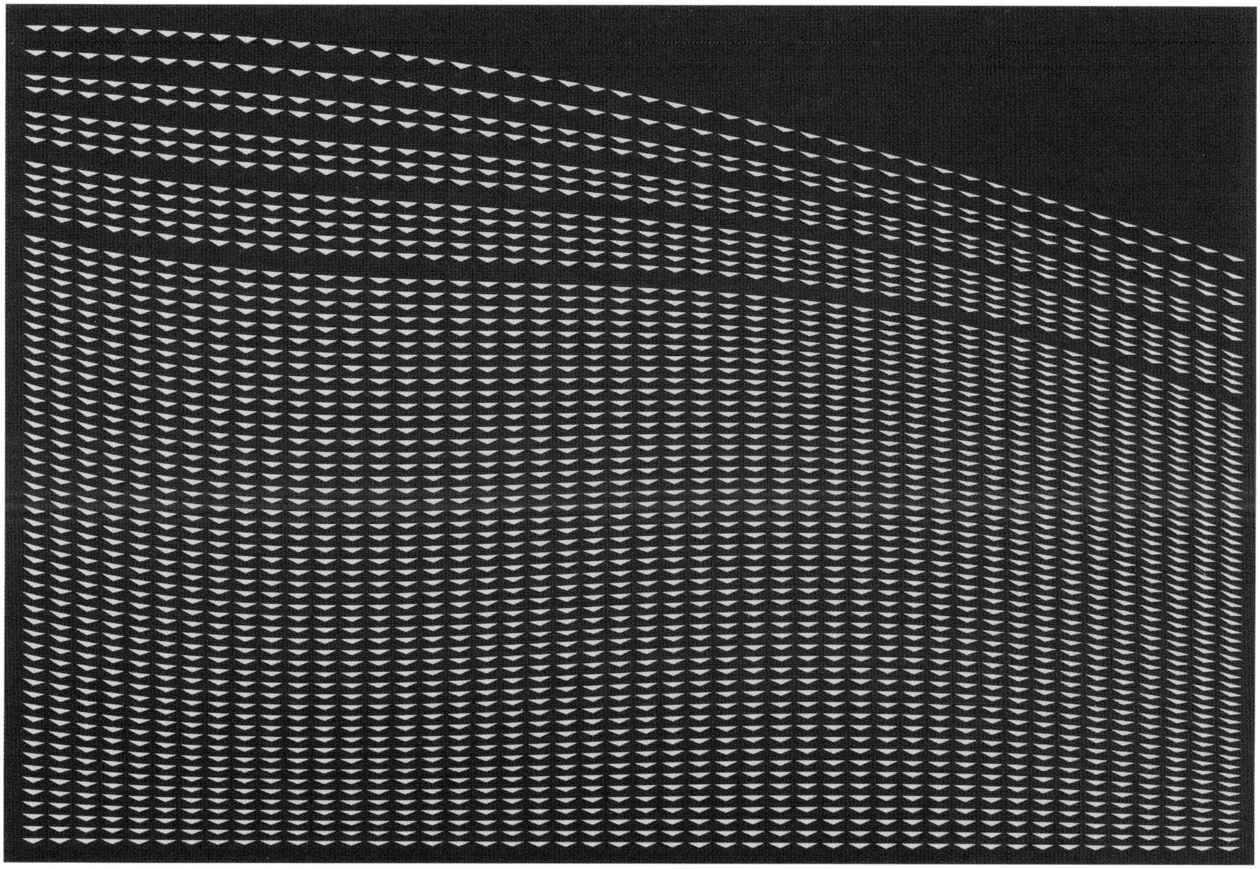

Eva Jiricna RA

Born: 3 March 1939, Zlin, Czechoslovakia
Elected RA: 19 May 1997
Category of Membership: Architect

Eva Jiricna studied at the University of Prague and the Prague Academy of Fine Arts. She was offered work experience at the Greater London Council and duly arrived in UK in July 1968. Three weeks later the Russians invaded Czechoslovakia and it was 22 years before she would return. From the GLC Architects' Department she moved to Louis de Soissons Partnership to work on the Brighton Marina project for ten years; from there to Richard Rogers' Partnership, collaborating on interior packages for the Lloyd's Building. She went on to form her own practice, Eva Jiricna Architects Limited, in 1985.

Jiricna's reputation and commissions went from strength to strength, notably in designing several award-winning outlets for the designer Joseph Ettedgui, developing the concept of 'lifestyle' retail and illustrating how shop design could be considered in an architectural manner. These were the boom years of retail and EJAL was commissioned by many other high-end companies. The practice designed Canada Water Bus Station, Rotherhithe, and the Kimberlin Library Extension in Leicester. A long-standing relationship with Boodles Jewellers has resulted in a string of Jiricna's designs across the UK, several featuring her 'signature' glass staircases, and the practice has completed many commercial and residential projects both here and abroad, as well as prestigious public buildings in the Czech Republic. Jiricna's appreciation for the modernist tradition that was so dominant in Czechoslovakia is evident in her work, manifesting itself in a respect and confidence in technology, the manufacturing process, and scrupulous attention to detail. Lightness and transparency are the hallmarks of her designs.

This whimsical drawing charts the convoluted trajectory of arriving at the end of a design process, illustrating the many setbacks as well as flashes of inspiration that arise out of dedicated team effort.

How We Do It, 2008
Pen on cartridge paper
45 × 64 cm

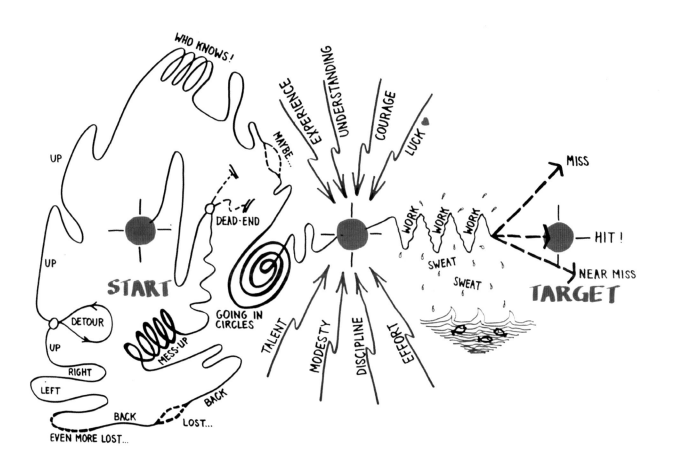

Allen Jones RA

Born: 1 September 1937, Southampton, Hampshire, UK
Elected ARA: 7 May 1981
Elected RA: 20 November 1986
Category of Membership: Printmaker

Allen Jones studied at Hornsey College of Art and the Royal College of Art in London. He has had an extensive teaching career in England, Germany and America and was a Trustee of the British Museum from 1990 to 1999. In 1963 he represented the UK at the Paris Biennale where he received the Prix des Jeunes Artistes. There have been three major retrospectives of his work, which have travelled around Britain and Germany, the last of which was shown at the Barbican before being toured worldwide by the British Council. His work is in many important collections including Tate, Hirschhorn, New York, Wallraf-Richartz Museum, Cologne, Moderna Museet, Stockholm, Stedelijk Museum, Amsterdam, and The

Museum of Modern Art, New York. He has designed for the Royal Ballet and Ballet Rambert, West Deutsche TV in Cologne and Thames TV in the UK. His sculptures have been commissioned for both private and public collections worldwide.

Together with Richard Hamilton, Peter Blake and R. B. Kitaj, Jones was one of the principal founders of British Pop Art. Eroticism has been a consistent theme in his paintings, sculptures and graphic works. In recent years this impulse has been focused on the figure of a nubile girl, which Jones realised was the exact same pose as the Degas *Petite danseuse*.

Enchanteresse has been produced on exactly the same scale as the little dancer in homage to Degas.

Enchanteresse, 2007
Bronze and leather with steel base
(edition of 8 with 4 artist proofs)
Figure 115 × 25 cm, base 81.3 × 60 cm

Anish Kapoor RA

Born: 12 March 1954, Bombay, India
Elected RA: 26 May 1999
Category of Membership: Sculptor

Anish Kapoor lives and works in London. He studied at Hornsey College of Art and went on to do postgraduate studies at the Chelsea School of Art. His first solo show was held in Paris in 1980, but his international reputation was soon established with a series of solo exhibitions held annually across the globe, including the Royal Academy of Art's major survey in 2009. Kapoor won the Turner Prize in 1991 and has been awarded Honorary Fellowships by the London Institute and Leeds University, University of Wolverhampton and the Royal Institute of British Architects. He has exhibited extensively all over the world and has designed celebrated public monuments, including *Cloud Gate* in Chicago and most recently *Orbit* for the Olympic Park, London, with Cecil Balmond.

Kapoor's sculptures arguably blur the boundaries between architecture, design and art with the treatment of form and the perception of space playing central roles. The interplay of polarities also provides a continuous thread throughout his body of work: form and light, external and internal, the solid and the intangible. His choice of sensual materials – pigment, stone, stainless steel and wax – combine with opulent colours, polished surfaces and optical effects of depth and dimension to beguile the viewer, inviting us to engage with the sculpture and evaluate our relationship with it.

The use of cement marks a new departure for Kapoor, and he constructed this piece by forcing concrete through a cement gun. This organic form of stacked spirals is at once elegant and curious, its pleats and folds suggesting growth and decay. Kapoor's works in cement have an incongruous quality; the piece is as unsettling as it is mesmerising.

Untitled, 2012
Cement
Height 55 cm

Anselm Kiefer Hon RA

Born: 8 March 1945, Donaueschingen, Germany
Elected Honorary RA: 29 May 1996

Anselm Kiefer lives in Paris and in a small village in the Black Forest near the border of France. Widely considered to be one of the most important European artists of the last few decades, his work has been collected and exhibited by major museums throughout the world. Alongside regular solo shows at Gagosian Gallery, White Cube and Thaddeus Ropac Gallery, he has had recent one-man exhibitions at Mass MoCA, Massachusetts, the Guggenheim Museum, Bilbao, the Royal Academy of Arts, London (2007), Louisiana Museum of Modern Art, Denmark (2010) and the Rijksmuseum, Amsterdam (2011). In 2007 he became the first living artist to have a work on permanent display at the Louvre since Georges Braque in 1953.

Kiefer is unafraid of confronting, questioning and drawing attention to history; he believes that 'only by going into the past can you go into the future'. Citing myth, poetry, music, landscape and religion, he has built up a deliberately indigenous set of subjects and symbols that are both aesthetically and intellectually

rigorous. Kiefer is a master of scale and perspective, and his work has a powerful physical presence that occupies a third space between painting, photography and sculpture that is entirely unique. Above all, perhaps, the frequently monumental works are about memory: how and why some things are remembered while others are allowed to dissipate. Fundamentally interested by human philosophical endeavour in the face of inexorable natural entropy and decay, his work has therefore increasingly explored cultures other than his own.

Here, the suspension of a medical tool above something as fluid and elemental as a seascape draws attention to mankind's constant desire to bring order to chaos, understanding to physical and emotional desires. The futility of our efforts is suggested by the rough exposure of the photograph to chemicals that will gradually change the work with merciless inevitability.

Des Meeres und der Liebe Wellen, 2011
Mixed media and gynaecological instrument on photographic paper
107 × 327 × 10 cm

Phillip King PPRA

Born: 1 May 1934, Tunis, Tunisia
Elected RA: 4 May 1988
President of the RA: 1995–2004
Category of Membership: Sculptor

Phillip King was born in Tunisia and came to England in 1945 to read modern languages at Cambridge University; it was here that he began to sculpt. He went on to study at St Martin's School of Art under the tutelage of Anthony Caro, and after graduating became an assistant to Henry Moore. In 1960 he was awarded the Boise scholarship and travelled to Greece to experience classical sculpture and architecture. His return to the UK was markedly dramatic – he destroyed all of his previous work, repainted his studio and started again. He established his reputation with group and solo exhibitions featuring works made from fibreglass, metal, wood and slate. He had retrospectives at the Whitechapel Gallery (1968), the Hayward Gallery (1981) and at Forte de Belvedere in Florence (1997) – King was only the second English sculptor to be given this honour following his mentor, Henry Moore.

King's early works are brutalist and surrealist in style. Small in scale, these robust sculptures were primarily made from clay and plaster. In the 1960s he experimented with colour and fibreglass, and it was during this period that he produced his seminal works: *Genghis Khan*, *Twilight* and *Rosebud* (all 1963). The 1980s saw him adopt a more figurative approach and he has recently returned to using colour in his work, which he has described as 'the life-line into this invisible world where feeling takes over from thinking'.

The Watcher is made from ceramic, a medium King experimented with in Japan and where he learnt to make ceramics on a large scale. It marks a move away from the use of industrial materials and the plinth and into the more immediate space of the viewer, a notion that is made all the more tangible by the somewhat sinister title of the piece. In spite of this, the sculpture is impish and somewhat traditional, suggesting itself to be part sentry, caryatid and water carrier. In this work King explores the spatial concerns of sculpture on a smaller scale.

The Watcher, 1995
Ceramic
Height 105 cm

Bryan Kneale RA

Born: 19 June 1930, Douglas, Isle of Man
Elected ARA: 23 April 1970
Elected RA: 12 February 1974
Category of Membership: Sculptor

The Manxman Bryan Kneale originally studied painting, first at Douglas School of Art (1947) and then at the Royal Academy Schools (1948–52). Aged 30 he moved from painting to sculpting and taught the subject at Horsey College of Art and Design, the Royal College of Art and the Royal Academy Schools. His first solo show of paintings was at the Redfern Gallery, London (1954). Other solo shows include a retrospective of his work at the Whitechapel Gallery (1966) and the Serpentine Gallery, London (1978). Group shows include 'Sculpture International' in Battersea Park (1963–6) and 'Chelsea Harbour Sculpture Show' (1993). He also curated and exhibited in 'British Sculptors' at the Royal Academy of Arts (1972) and the Jubilee Exhibition of British Sculpture, Battersea Park (1977).

Kneale works primarily in metal, creating free-form sculptures that focus largely on the way separate elements are joined and combined: the writer Hilary Spurling has described his work as 'line drawings in space'. Spun steel and aluminium domes are dissected and realigned to create curvaceous wall and floor-based pieces, their surfaces burnished, painted or patinated. 'I think all my work is about the problem of what one sees and what one knows and the attempt to fuse the two, and in a special sense disrupt them,' says the artist.

Tarquinia is a town northwest of Rome, perhaps a reference to Kneale's time in Italy after receiving a Rome Scholarship in painting from the Royal Academy Schools. It was during this period that he was influenced by the Futurists and the metaphysical painting movement. Though smaller than many of his pieces, *Tarquinia* demonstrates Kneale's interest in shape; it is as much about the negative space between the copper sheets as it is about the solid form. 'Even in my most abstract work I've always searched for a persona in order to feel the work has a life of its own.'

Tarquinia, 2000
Copper
Height 48 cm

Jeff Koons Hon RA

Born: 21 January 1955, York, Pennsylvania, USA
Elected Honorary RA: 16 March 2010

Jeff Koons studied at the Maryland Institute College of Art in Baltimore, and after an exchange year at the School of the Art Institute in Chicago he graduated in 1976. His work is found in numerous public collections including the Guggenheim Museum, New York/Bilbao, Tate, Stedelijk Museum, Amsterdam and the Museum of Contemporary Art, Tokyo. Most recently he has had several survey shows at major venues internationally including the Metropolitan Museum of Art, New York, Tate Modern, Scottish National Gallery of Modern Art, Edinburgh, the Museum of Contemporary Art, Chicago, and the Palace of Versailles. Concurrent painting and sculpture exhibitions opened this year at Liebieghaus Skulpturensammlung and Schirn Kunsthalle, Frankfurt. Recent awards include the Officier de la Legion d'Honneur and the John Singleton Copley Award from the RA.

Koons' work synthesises the concerns of Conceptual and Pop art with contemporary mass culture to create iconographic painting and sculpture that are simultaneously monumental, familiar, witty and often controversial. Borrowing from a distinctly American set of conventional values he elevates unexpected objects to art status in an echo of the Duchampian tradition: for example vacuum cleaners encased in Perspex, domestic products and toys replicated as tributes to sterility and consumption. Koons uses the best of digital technology and craftsmanship to achieve exquisitely finished works that hide all traces of their fabrication.

Monkey Train forms a part of his 2007 *Hulk-Elvis* series. Koons says the monkey's face is a reference to Picabia's *Portrait of Cézanne*. 'This painting is about everyone. The train in the background meeting the horse and buggy is a reference to Darwinism. One technology replacing the other is really a sexual tension. The painting is about our own mortality, feeling very much in the moment but conscious of both our past and our future.'

Monkey Train, 2007
Silkscreen with archival pigmented inkjet on Somerset paper (edition of 40 plus 10 artist's proofs)
83.5 × 66.3 cm

Paul Koralek RA

Born: 7 April 1933, Vienna, Austria
Elected ARA: 19 May 1986
Elected RA: 26 June 1991
Category of Membership: Architect

Paul Koralek studied architecture at the Architectural Association, London from 1951. Like the school, Koralek was very cosmopolitan; he was born in Vienna and studied in Paris for a year. While at the AA he teamed up with two fellow students, Peter Ahrends and Richard Burton, and they have been associated together ever since. They set up their practice – Ahrends Burton and Koralek (ABK) – in 1961 and today it is based in Dublin. Before this however, Koralek worked for the late Philip Powell RA and also for the great Modernist Marcel Breuer.

Koralek says architecture 'is about people and their lives, about making spaces that will have a living dynamic, a significant relationship with the life and activity that they will contain'. Trained in the epoch of Modernist architecture, Koralek is nonconformist in his approach. He thrives on designing buildings for unusual spaces, embracing the challenges they present.

Koralek won a competition in 1960 to design the Berkeley Library at Trinity College Dublin, the first of many commissions for TCD and in Dublin in general. It was this first project that enabled ABK to open an office in that city. This drawing shows a design development study for the Dublin Dental Hospital, part of the university's campus. Dealing with an important city site and the juxtaposition of his design with an older building, Koralek again showed his interest in the relationship between form and use, creating a site that was aesthetically pleasing but which also delivered the technical and functional needs of the hospital.

Dublin Dental Hospital: Design Development Study, 1994
Pencil on paper
21 × 29.7 cm

Michael Landy RA

Born: 5 May 1963, London, UK
Elected RA: 29 May 2008
Category of Membership: Painter

Michael Landy's appeal as an artist is an unusual blend of big ideas – on consumerism, the value of humanity in a corporate rubric and the commodification of art – and technical skill in precise botanical drawing and intimate portraiture. He trained at Loughborough College of Art and Goldsmiths College in London. In 1999 his work was included in the seminal 'Sensation' exhibition at the Royal Academy of Arts, alongside Damien Hirst and Tracey Emin who Landy had met at Goldsmiths.

Whereas Hirst has gone on to challenge the limits of the value of art, Landy has questioned how little everyday possessions are worth. He most famously explored this in *Break Down* (2001) in which in collaboration with Artangel, and as a satire on consumerism, he took over an empty C&A store on Oxford Street and proceeded to catalogue and then methodically destroy all of his possessions.

Another iconic work was *Semi-Detached* in which Landy minutely recorded and then recreated his parents' quotidian home inside Tate Britain. Again the work was a 'process' that awoke in Landy a profound affection for his parents and in particular his father. It was an unflinching portrayal of real life. Similarly, following successful cancer treatment to remove a testicle, Landy drew a pragmatic and characteristically brave self-portrait, shown at the Wellcome Collection.

This whimsical work details an imagined mechanical scene in his signature scrawling lines, suggestive of mad-cap invention and subversive ideas. The monochrome palette adds to the dream-like atmosphere, as if the scene is illuminated by moonlight. It is part of a series responding to Jean Tinguely's *Joyous Machines* — eccentric sculptures that explored the same themes of construction and destruction — and is based on a photographic still of Tinguely's seminal artwork *Homage to New York*. In October 2009 Landy co-curated a joint retrospective of Tinguely and himself at Tate Liverpool.

H.2.N.Y. Ying is Yang, 2006
Gouache and glue on paper
66.5 × 101.5 cm

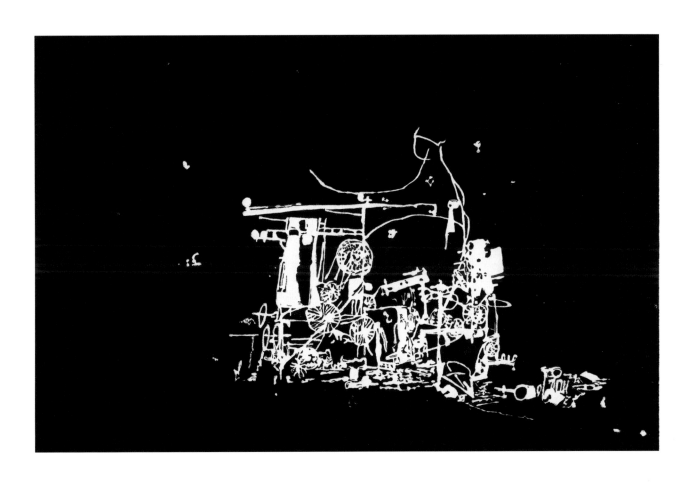

Sonia Lawson RA

Born: 2 June 1934, Darlington, Durham, UK
Elected ARA: 6 May 1982
Elected RA: 26 June 1991
Category of Membership: Painter

Sonia Lawson studied at Doncaster School of Art and the Royal College of Art, London. She has taught at a number of institutions throughout her career including Harrow School of Art, West Surrey College of Art, St Martin's School of Art and Design and the Royal College of Art. She was a visiting lecturer at the Royal Academy Schools from 1985 to 2006. Lawson's first solo exhibition was held at the Zwemmer Gallery in London (1960), with subsequent shows at the Trafford Gallery, Manchester City Art Gallery and the Wakeford Gallery in West Yorkshire, as well as a number of group exhibitions throughout the UK, Switzerland, China and the USA.

Lawson's work deals largely with 'personal truths and experiences' underscored by an energy drawn from her native northern landscape. 'Good drawing always transcends those trends which beset painting and other forms of visual expression within any period,' she explains. 'It is a most personal revelation,

the DNA, the proof one way or another of calibre. Good drawing is never just about craft or virtuoso skills, nor the dogged science that leads to feats of portrayal. It is about a show of warmth and understanding, a sensitivity and genuine engagement with subject. It is about discovery, awareness and articulacy and it is the core of creativity.'

In *Twin Forms* Lawson evades topographical constraints. It is a poetic image that challenges the spectator on several levels. The emphasis here is seemingly on the symbolism of the pared-down female form, amplified by the curves of a cello, but, placed on the canvas with a second female figure lying beneath, this is not simply an allusion to the classical nude. Instead it becomes an expression of the tension between opposites – the drawn figure on the canvas, the reclining figure beneath her and the figure of the viewer.

Twin Forms, 2003
Silkscreen: 3 colours
60 × 48 cm

Christopher Le Brun PRA

Born: 20 December 1951, Portsmouth, Hampshire, UK
Elected RA: 12 December 1996
Elected President of the RA: 8 December 2011
Category of Membership: Engraver

Christopher Le Brun is a painter, sculptor and printmaker. He is the 26th President of the Royal Academy since Sir Joshua Reynolds and the youngest to be elected since Lord Leighton in 1878.

He trained at the Slade and Chelsea Schools of Art in London, and appeared early on in many group exhibitions, such as the influential Zeitgeist exhibition at the Martin-Gropius-Bau, Berlin, and from 1980 in many solo exhibitions in Britain, Europe and America including a survey at the Astrup Fearnley Museum of Modern Art, Oslo (1995). He was a prizewinner at the John Moores Liverpool exhibitions in 1978 and 1980 and worked in Berlin during 1987–8 as guest of the DAAD artist's programme.

Between 1990 and 2003 he served as a Trustee of Tate and subsequently of the National Gallery, a period which saw his involvement in the creation of Tate Modern, as well as the masterplan and re-development of the east wing of the National Gallery. In recent years he has been a trustee of the Prince's Drawing School,

which he helped to establish in 2000. In the same year he was elected as the Royal Academy's first Professor of Drawing.

At a time when artists frequently use traditional modes or quotations in a spirit of irony, the repertoire of motifs with which his work is especially associated makes patent his strong attachment to the imagery and emotional address of Romanticism and Symbolism.

Although the central motif in *Gulf* is the horse, it is not its subject. The image of the horse not only refers to how it has been employed in Western art as a representation of grace, power and nobility, but also acts as an anchor for the act of painting itself. The motif attracts our attention, confronts us and returns our gaze, but it is there first and foremost as a poetic symbol. His paintings ask us to attend not only to the compelling imagery he employs, but also to the poetic and structural processes through which it is made visible.

Gulf, 2012
Oil on canvas
240 × 170 cm

Richard Long RA

Born: 2 June 1945, Bristol, UK
Elected RA: 5 December 2001
Category of Membership: Sculptor

Thrown out of the West of England College of Art in 1965 for being 'too precocious', Richard Long completed his artistic education at St Martin's School of Art, London. While there he made a quietly revolutionary work, *A Line Made by Walking* (1967), that marked the beginning of a career that has been celebrated in numerous international exhibitions and awards. Recent solo shows include Haunch of Venison, London and Berlin, San Francisco Museum of Modern Art (2006), Scottish National Gallery of Modern Art, Edinburgh (2007), the Musée d'Art Moderne et d'Art Contemporain, Nice (2008) and Tate Britain (2009). The Turner Prize (1989) and the Praemium Imperiale Prize for Sculpture (2009) are among his many accolades.

Using the most fundamental of materials and sculptural forms, Long has redefined the parameters of what we consider to be sculpture. *A Line Made by Walking*, a photograph of a straight patch of grass flattened by the tread of Long's feet in a field near

London, was premised on the notion that the journey itself could be art. This belief has remained at the heart of Long's work; he makes landscape sculptures that 'inhabit the rich territory between two ideological positions', namely that of making 'monuments' or conversely of 'leaving only footprints'. He has said he has no desire to make lasting, recognisable monuments because it is the action of a walk, the relocation of a stone, or the splash of mud on a wall or a found object that is the sculpture – landscape is both his medium and his subject. 'The idea that no one sees it is part of the work,' he has said. 'I can make it in a very remote place, almost secretly.'

As well as leaving and recording traces and marks of passage, another category of the artist's work is drawing: papers dipped in watery mud, or mud fingerprints on driftwood. *Niger Drawing* is more untypical, being a washboard found in a West African market, and later marked with black paint, transforming a human object from one use to another.

Niger Drawing, 2009
Wood
40 × 20 × 2 cm

Richard MacCormac RA

Born: 3 September 1938, London, UK
Elected RA: 24 May 1993
Category of Membership: Architect

From the early stages of what was to become an illustrious career, Richard MacCormac reflected the distinct educational experiences of Cambridge University and the Bartlett School of Architecture at UCL, the former representing the cultural aspirations of architecture, the latter its pragmatic and social obligations. Like many architects of his generation, his early experience of practice was in the public sector, working on housing schemes for the London Borough of Merton and in Milton Keynes.

The Sainsbury Building – MacCormac's bold addition to Worcester College – represents a shift away from the purely pragmatic towards an architecture that draws, simultaneously, on the language of the modern movement and that of traditional architecture. It led to a series of college projects, notably for St John's College Oxford and Trinity College Cambridge.

This shift also heralded MacCormac's quest for a broader sense of architectural meaning, particularly in the relationship between art and architecture. His design for the Ruskin Library at the University of Lancaster was the ideal commission, allowing him to reference and explore Ruskin's place in art history via the materials and composition of his contemporary building. MacCormac has also pursued his passion in this field with his exhibition designs at both Tate Britain and Tate Modern and his work with the Phoenix Initiative, where he collaborated with artists to draw together ideas from art and architecture to build a future for central Coventry. This commitment is also reflected in his role as chair of the RA Forum.

This architectural drawing of the Sainsbury Building illustrates how the new building creates a transition between the city and the secret domain of the college park. The three storeys of student rooms around shared kitchens interweave with each other, blend with the surrounding trees and are reflected in the water of the lake.

The Sainsbury Building, Worcester College, Oxford – Diagonal Section, 1980
Ink and pencil on tracing paper
59.4 × 84.1 cm

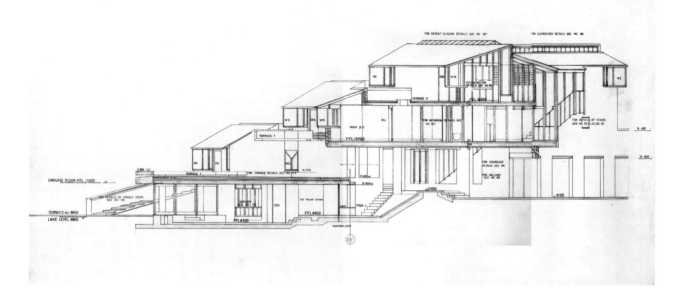

FOR PATENT GLAZING DETAILS SEE WC 187

FOR CLERESTORY DETAILS SEE WC 188

KITCHEN UNIT FOR
DETAILS SEE WC 164

TERRACE 11

FFL 18250

FOR BATHROOM DETAILS SEE
WC 124

FOR DETAILS OF STAIRS
SEE WC 115,91,92,93,39

ROOM B12

D11

TERRACE 7

FFL 13700

N 400

12 600

FOR STAIRCASE
DETAILS SEE WC

FOR HALLWAY
SEE WC 187

10400

11.775

GROUND FLOOR FFL 15000

TERRACE 3

FOR TERRACE DETAILS SEE WC 173

10550

FOR DETAILS OF DINKEY STEPS
SEE WC 195

STAIR 3

TERRACE NO1 8950

LAKE LEVEL 8800

FFL 8950

FFL 8500

expansion joint

David Mach RA

Born: 18 March 1956, Methil, Fife, Scotland, UK
Elected RA: 21 May 1998
Category of Membership: Sculptor

David Mach studied at Duncan of Jordanstone College of Art, Dundee, and at the Royal College of Art, London. He then lectured at Kingston University for four years as well as at the Contemporary Art Summer School, Kitakyushu, Japan. In 1999 he was appointed Visiting Professor at the Sculpture Department, Edinburgh College of Art. Mach's first solo exhibition was held at the Lisson Gallery in 1982 and since then he has had solo and group exhibitions across the world. As well as being awarded numerous major commissions, he was nominated for the Turner Prize (1988) and won the Lord Provost's Prize in Glasgow (1992). In his largest solo show to date, at Edinburgh City Art Centre last year, Mach used sculpture, collage and text to explore the themes and legacy of the King James Bible.

Mach is known for his highly inventive sculptures and collages that are generally created from found materials and mass-produced objects such as matchsticks, coat hangers and postcards. Always intricate and very often on an impressively large scale, Mach has portrayed modern life in a spectrum that ranges from animals to machines to cartoons. His ability to capture contemporary society was perhaps most memorably demonstrated in *The National Portrait*, a collage measuring 3 x 70 m and featuring thousands of images of the British people at work and at play, commissioned for the Millennium Dome.

Mr Right and Miss Wong, comprising hundreds of postcards of a beaming Prince William, is a strong example of how Mach cleverly combines current popular culture with great technical skill to make a humorous and visually arresting artwork.

Mr Right and Miss Wong, 2009
Postcard collage
182.9 × 182.9 cm

John Maine RA

Born: 31 October 1942, Bristol, UK
Elected RA: 22 May 1995
Category of Membership: Sculptor

John Maine studied at the West of England College of Art and the Royal College of Art, London. He held the first fellowship at the Yorkshire Sculpture Park, with a solo show in 1978. He has shown regularly in Britain, including the Hayward Gallery (1991), British Museum (2003) and Royal Academy of Arts (2011).

Maine has travelled widely, carving in many quarries and stoneyards, gaining expertise by studying different traditions and materials. He worked with Japanese sculptors and masons in 1980 to create an environmental stone landscape in Yamaguchi Prefecture. In 1993 he returned to Japan to make a 10 metre-high granite sculpture for the completion of the Ryugasaki New Town Development in Iberaki. He worked for a year in Australia, carving a granite sculpture for the British High Commission in Canberra, and visited Bhopal in India to make *Observatory*. His large-scale stone installations can be seen across Britain, such as *Arena* by the National Theatre on London's South Bank, his memorial sculpture in

Islington Green (2006) and *Sea Strata* (2012) at Green Park Underground. Recently his interest in geology has led to several major coastal projects, working with marine engineers on land retention and sea defences. He has been a member of the Cathedrals Fabric Commission for England (1993–2011) and is currently a member of the Westminster Abbey Fabric Commission and the Fabric Advisory Committees of St George's Chapel Windsor, and Norwich Cathedral.

The insight he has gained as an advisor for the conservation of the Cosmati Pavement in Westminster Abbey has taken him in a new direction. Laid in 1268 at the foot of the Shrine of St Edward the Confessor, this enigmatic mosaic is based on a geometric design formed of a sequence of roundels. Maine was inspired by the apparent simplicity of the design that belies its underlying complexity. *Interwoven* pays homage and beautifully suggests a macrocosm through microcosms of intricate detail.

Interwoven, 2011
Incised Indian granite
59.8 × 61.8 × 2 cm

Leonard Manasseh RA

Born: 21 May 1916, Singapore
Elected ARA: 30 April 1976
Elected RA: 9 May 1979
Category of Membership: Architect

Since he began his practice in 1950 Leonard Manasseh has had a stylistic commitment to the lines and shapes of modernism, without severity or austerity. His clever economy with materials is typical of the philosophy of the Hertfordshire County Council where he worked in the Architects department from 1946 (after three years in the Fleet Air Arm) and his studies at the Architectural Association. As post-war austerity fell away he added depth to his designs, but his work has retained a legacy of function, simplicity and the graphic lines of modernism.

This 1964 painterly pen-and-wash drawing details designs for the interior of a restaurant. This was the realm in which Manasseh first made his name; he came to an admiring public's attention with his design for the Festival of Britain restaurant. His commitment to the uncompromising geometry of modernism is in evidence in this stylish drawing, but so too is a delicacy and sense of timelessness. Indeed, it was being both of his time – and distanced from it – that equipped Manasseh with a talent for modernist designs within historic contexts. This aspect of his practise included a collaboration with the landscape architect Elizabeth Chesterton on a study for King's Lynn, now a textbook example of mastering dual architectural impulses of regeneration and preservation.

Hook, Line and Sinker, 1964
Pen and wash on paper
60 × 85 cm

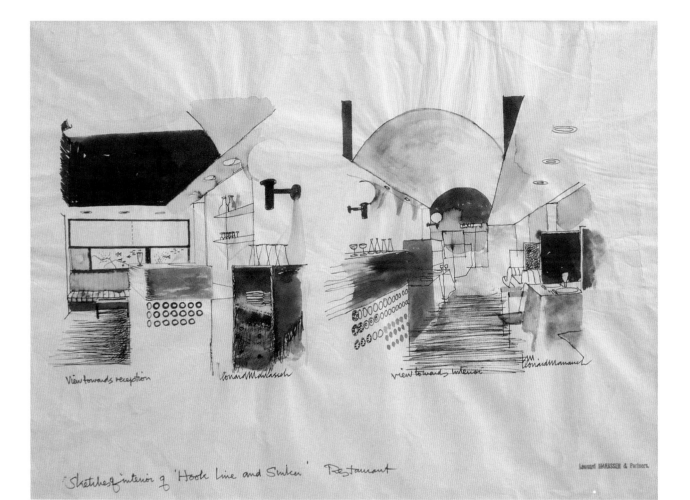

View towards reception   Leonard Manasseh   view towards interior   Leonard Manasseh

'Sketches of interior of 'Hook Line and Sinker' Restaurant

Leonard MANASSEH & Partners.

Michael Manser RA

Born: 23 March 1929, London, UK
Elected RA: 8 November 1994
Category of Membership: Architect

Michael Manser set up his own architectural practice in 1961 following studies at Regent's Street Polytechnic and a period working in London and the West Indies. He has since gained widespread recognition as an educator, writer and innovator in the profession, winning multiple awards over the last five decades for his private, public and commercial projects. He has written extensively on architecture for *Architectural Design* and the *Observer*, and he regularly acts as an awards consultant for public projects. He was President of the Royal Institute of British Architects (RIBA) from 1983 to 1985.

Manser has contributed to the popularity of contemporary design by helping to mediate between the voices of traditionalism in British architecture and advocates of a more progressive aesthetic. In his work and in his writing he has made it clear how a fusion of traditional materials and sensitivity to context and function allows modern design to create successful built solutions. His design for the Hilton Hotel at Heathrow Terminal 4 exemplifies this: completed in 1990 for BAA by the Manser Practice, this £32 million project took less than 27 months from commencement of design to occupation. Making a powerful formal statement out of a transitory space, Manser grouped together the 400 rooms of the hotel into one large, offset rectangle, allowing a vast, light-filled atrium to be at its heart. Its bold simplicity has contributed both to the hotel's low running costs and high profitability, and earned it a reputation as a future classic. Its success was acknowledged with multiple awards across several fields in 1991, including the UK RIBA Award Winner, the Royal Fine Art Commission Building of the Year Award and the British Construction Industry Awards Winner.

The Queen's Suite, Heathrow Airport, 1988
One-off print from the original drawing
50 × 70 cm

Michael Manser RA

Leonard McComb RA

Born: 3 August 1930, Glasgow, Scotland, UK
Elected ARA: 27 May 1987
Elected RA: 26 June 1991
Category of Membership: Draughtsman

Leonard McComb is a painter, draughtsman, printmaker and sculptor. He studied at Manchester School of Art and the Slade School of Fine Art, London, and went on to teach at the latter, as well as Oxford Brookes University, Sir John Cass College, Royal College of Art and Goldsmiths College. In 1974 he founded the Sunningwell School of Art, Oxford. McComb has undertaken many public and private commissions. In 1999 he completed a commissioned portrait of the novelist Doris Lessing for the National Portrait Gallery, and the following year he was selected by the Vatican to design a Jubilee Medal to commemorate the Millennium. His work is held in many public collections including those of the Arts Council, British Council, British Museum, Cambridge University, Manchester Art Gallery, National Portrait Gallery, Tate and the Victoria and Albert Museum.

McComb describes his finely observed drawings, oils, watercolours, prints and sculpture as visual abstractions after nature. He is preoccupied by details, and thinks of every art work – whether it be a figure, a landscape, flower or still-life – as a portrait. This stems from McComb's belief that nature's 'forms and shapes radiate from a centre. This may be described as a tension; the anthropologists call it Mana. It is the name given to that force immanent in all things, not merely men and animals, but even inanimate objects like rocks and sticks – an elemental force manifested universally.' This skilful and careful drawing of the horse exhibited at the RA in 1979 shows McComb's technical prowess and sensitivity to his subject. Despite the age and artificiality of the bronze, he has managed to capture something of a horse's vivacity and spirit in these drawings. This iconic sculpture was clearly important to the young artist, for he later made etchings based on these sketches.

Drawings of the bronze horse from the Basilica of St Mark's in Venice on exhibition at the Royal Academy in 1979, 1979
Pencil on handmade paper
61 × 62 cm

Jock McFadyen RA

Born: 18 September 1950, Paisley, Scotland, UK
Elected RA: 24 May 2012
Category of Membership: Painter

Jock McFadyen studied at Chelsea School of Art, London, and sold his first painting to Allen Jones in 1974. During the 1970s he gained recognition for schematic, witty, narrative paintings.

In 1981 McFadyen was appointed artist-in-residence at the National Gallery in London, during which time his work changed direction and he became more interested in painting what he saw around him, rather than participating in a conceptual dialogue surrounding art's own history. Following a commission in 1992 to design the sets and costumes for Kenneth MacMillan's 'The Judas Tree' at the Royal Opera House, the figures that had been dominant in his work up until that point disappeared, leaving the haunting landscapes the artist is celebrated for today.

McFadyen respects painting as a sophisticated way of describing the world, finding its unique capacity for scale, depth of field, focus and pictorial experimentation exhilarating. While the restrained, painterly integrity of his paintings may speak of his admiration for Whistler, Sickert and Lowry, he sees his pictures as having more in common with stories or songs about the landscape than current painting. His delicate handling of stark, urban landscapes creates strikingly atmospheric pictures.

Novelist Iain Sinclair's response to McFadyen's 2001 exhibition resonates with this painting particularly well: '… A post-nuclear clarity. Fault lines radiating out from monster boards onto the camber of the road.' *Looking West* shows how paintings, like stories, allow invention to coexist with intelligent observation.

McFadyen's work is held in over 30 public collections including Tate, Museum of London and the National Gallery. This year his work has been shown as part of the Edinburgh Art Festival, the Fine Art Society and at the Fleming Collection, London. Upcoming exhibitions include Eleven Spitalfields, London.

Looking West, 2003
Oil on canvas
122 × 183 cm

Lisa Milroy RA

Born: 16 January 1959, Vancouver, Canada
Elected RA: 13 December 2005
Category of Membership: Painter

Lisa Milroy was born in Vancouver and graduated from Goldsmiths College, London, in 1983. She has exhibited her paintings across the UK and abroad, and her work is included in many private and public collections. She has been Head of Graduate Painting at Slade School of Fine Art since 2009.

Still-life is at the heart of Milroy's practice. In the 1980s her paintings featured ordinary objects isolated against an off-white ground, such as shoes, clothes, books, light bulbs and hardware. In the early 1990s Milroy's approach to still-life painting shifted, leading to depictions of objects within settings. As the imagery expanded to include landscape, architecture and people, her painting style diversified. By continually experimenting with fast and slow applications of paint, she has achieved within her paintings a wide range of moods and atmospheres.

In recent years Milroy's focus has been on installation-based paintings. In January 2012 she presented *Act One, Seen Too* at the Bloomsbury Theatre, London, a painting designed for theatre space. Components of the painting were arranged on the stage, which viewers experienced from both the auditorium and stage itself. This exploration of the participatory nature of painting and the relation between object and image led to a group of 'objectpaintings' entitled *Wearable Paintings*, which included *Shirt*. Cut, sewn and painted, this shirt cannot be worn, but stirs the imagination to transform the collection of marks and materials into something that prompts questions about presence, absence and identity: clothes are animated when they are worn, and perform differently depending on the wearer. Do they therefore become a part of the self? Are they less real when not being worn? Milroy's paintings suggest that our selves are touched by and made up of the objects that surround us.

Shirt, 2011
Acrylic on fabric, black thread, buttons, wooden hanger
75 × 66 cm

Dhruva Mistry RA

Born: 1 January 1957, Kanjari, Gujarat, India
Elected ARA: 29 May 1991
Elected RA: 26 June 1991
Category of Membership: Sculptor

Dhruva Mistry was born in Gujarat, India. He studied at the Faculty of Fine Arts in Baroda, before moving to the Royal College of Art in London on a British Council Scholarship. In 1984–5 he was artist-in-residence at Kettle's Yard, Cambridge, and has since shown regularly throughout the UK and abroad. He was sculptor-in-residence at the Victoria and Albert Museum, London, represented Britain at the Third Rodin Grand Prize Exhibition in Japan and was also selected for the show 'Asian Artists Today' at the Fukuoka Art Museum. In 1992 he was commissioned to design sculptures for Victoria Square, Birmingham, for which he received several awards. He lives and works in Vadodara.

Best known for his sculptures, Mistry combines religious art of ancient civilisations with the popular art of the bazaar. His work bears a rich narrative quality and varies in style and scale – from small sculptures, maquettes and wall reliefs, to monumental pieces for public spaces made of sand, cement, stone and stainless steel. It encompasses influences of Egyptian and Cycladic art, Hinduism and Buddhism, while also referencing European traditions of figurative sculpture.

In *Spatial Diagram 06 (Vermillion)* Mistry employs a contemporary re-working of the language of Cubism. The sculpture is defined in terms of planes, forms and cut-outs. He plays with the viewer's perceptions as they are invited to explore the sculpture by looking at it, into it, round it and through it. The shape of the sculpture changes with every angle, and so too does the nature of the steel, as its smooth, unblemished surface responds to different lights, shadows and reflections.

Spatial Diagram 06 (Vermillion), 2004–06
Stainless steel and paint
31 × 31 × 27.5 cm

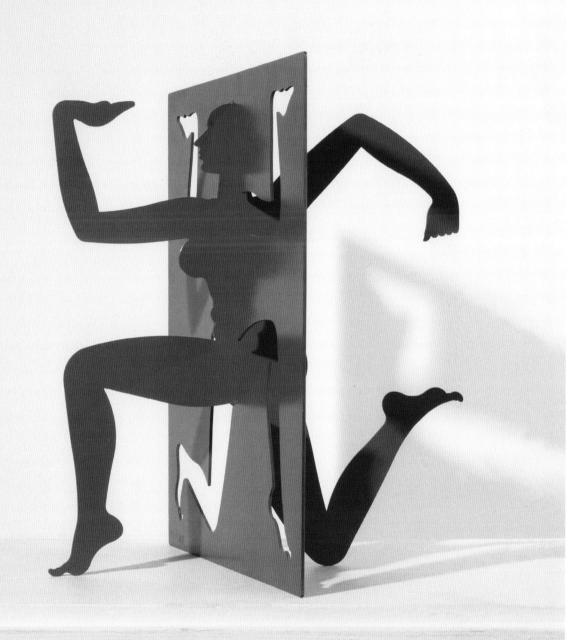

Mick Moon RA

Born: 9 November 1937, Edinburgh, Scotland, UK
Elected RA: 23 May 1994
Category of Membership: Printmaker

Mick Moon was born in Scotland and studied in London at Chelsea School of Art followed by a year at the Royal College of Art. Between 1973 and 1990 he was Senior Lecturer at the Slade School of Fine Art, London, except for a year spent as artist-in-residence at the Prahran School of Art and Design in Melbourne, Australia, in 1982. Many of his solo shows, including his first in 1969, were held at Waddington Galleries, London, but he has also shown at Tate Britain (1976), Ikon Gallery, Birmingham (1980), Macquaire Galleries, Sydney (1982), Dolan Maxwell Gallery, Philadelphia (1986) and at the Bowles Sorokko Gallery, San Francisco (1996) among others. He has received many awards including a major Arts Council award (1980) and first prize at the John Moores Liverpool exhibition (1984).

Moon is a painter and a printmaker. He often explores unusual techniques to create his works and is interested in the concept of layering, as can be seen in his many collages. He has a particular interest in artists such as Cézanne and Bonnard as well as in Cubism.

Moon created this monotype by pressing down a wet, painted canvas onto a board that he has pre-painted. Having added a small layer of wet paint to this board so that the two will slowly stick together as they dry, he then rips one away from the other, leaving the swirly, graffiti-like background in the image. The jar, collaged over the top, is one of many objects Moon collected in India; it creates a focal point in the image that most would recognise as a still-life, but which the artist prefers to call an interior. The orange liquid represented in the bottom of the jar creates a serene contrast with the chaotic background. Titled *The Last Drop*, it adds an element of intrigue and curiosity for the viewer who might wonder what exactly it could be.

The Last Drop, 1994
Monotype with collage
49.2 × 40.6 cm

Mali Morris RA

Born: 5 February 1945, Caernarfon, North Wales, UK
Elected: 16 March 2010
Category of Membership: Painter

Mali Morris studied Fine Art at the University of Newcastle upon Tyne and the University of Reading. Her first major solo exhibitions were at the Serpentine Gallery, London, and Ikon Gallery, Birmingham, in the late 1970s. She has shown extensively since then in over 30 solo shows and many group exhibitions in the UK and overseas. Her work is in private and public collections worldwide, including the Arts Council England, British Council, Contemporary Arts Society, Government Art Collection, Museum of Wales, Cardiff, and the Whitworth Art Gallery, Manchester.

Painting is a two-fold experience for Morris: both an expressive act and a continuous contemplation about what art is. She is acutely aware of how painting's history shows its contemporary possibilities. Her luminous and highly concentrated artworks have an apparent immediacy, an invitation to participate in their complex and constantly unfolding pictorial structures.

'*Back to Front* is a recent work from an ongoing series, in which I bury colour with colour, and then excavate it, finding new relationships as I go. The first layers of the painting, covered over and now retrieved (in this case at the four corners), come up to the front, but the eye returns instinctively into pictorial space. Luminosity constructed through colour emanates into real space. These movements in and out of the painting are some of the contradictions that keep it alive, and offer paradox. That's one of the things I'm looking for, in an image which tells of its making. Finding it is how I decide when a painting is finished, but the idea of painting is never finished.'

Back to Front, 2012
Acrylic on canvas
50 × 60 cm

David Nash RA

Born: 14 November 1945, Esher, Surrey, UK
Elected RA: 26 May 1999
Category of Membership: Sculptor

David Nash studied at Kingston College of Art and Chelsea School of Art (Postgraduate). His first solo exhibitions were held in 1973 at York's Queen Elizabeth Hall and at Oriel in Bangor, Wales. These led to a series of solo exhibitions throughout the UK and his international reputation was cemented in 1980 with his first solo shows abroad in New York and Venice. He has continued to exhibit on an annual basis worldwide.

Nash assumes a responsive and adaptable approach to creating art, allowing his environment to determine the direction his creations will take. The forces of nature play a central role in his sculptures and he is perhaps best known for his work in unseasoned timber: 'There's a profound wisdom there, stretching over millennia,' he explains. 'I take my cue from what the material suggests to me.' 'Wood is elemental: it naturally grows out of the elements and engages with them.' Some works are made using fire and charring, while others are living or planted, such as *Ash Dome*, a circle of trees carefully trained into a dome shape using hedge-laying skills. It was not until 1999 that Nash began working in bronze.

This bronze sculpture *Cross Hatch Column* still holds echoes of his work in wood; it bears the same essential form and geometry of carved vertical, horizontal and diagonal cuts that are so often identifying features of his work. Smaller than many of his wood sculptures, a sense of mass is still evoked as the structure juts skywards, while the bronze patina is resonant of smoke and ash. Like much of his work *Cross Hatch Column* seems fundamentally collaborative – an expression of the relationship between the artist, his material and the natural world.

Cross Hatch Column, 2011
Bronze
Height 68 cm

Humphrey Ocean RA

Born: 22 June 1951, Pulborough, Sussex, UK
Elected RA: 26 May 2004
Category of Membership: Painter

Humphrey Ocean studied at art schools in Tunbridge Wells, Brighton and Canterbury. In 1982 he won the Imperial Tobacco Portrait Award (now the BP Portrait Award) and went on to establish himself as a leading portrait painter. His first solo show was at the National Portrait Gallery and many of his commissions are now in its collection. His time in Brazil with the American anthropologist Stephen Nugent culminated in the book *Big Mouth: The Amazon Speaks*, and in 1992 Ocean's collaboration with the scientist and filmmaker John Tchalenko was shown in 'Double-Portrait' at Tate Liverpool. In 2002 he was artist-in-residence at Dulwich Picture Gallery and had solo shows there, as well as at Sidney Cooper Gallery, Canterbury (2009) and Jesus College, Cambridge (2011). He was made Professor of Perspective at the Royal Academy of Arts this year, and in autumn 2012 a series of new portraits 'A Handbook of Modern Life' will be displayed at the National Portrait Gallery, accompanied by a book.

The title of Ocean's Canterbury exhibition was 'Perfectly Ordinary'. As well as portraits he paints the familiar, and what some would call the unremarkable: the view through his windscreen, a suburban house, passengers on the tube. He paints what we know, but often these are the very things that are ignored. By making them his subject Ocean renders them visible, and invites us to share in his fascination with the fact that almost all of what we see has been created by us. *Tangerine Static* presents a household object before us so we can look and think about it properly, without being distracted by its function or ubiquity. Although direct and dispassionate, it is surprising and faintly comical. Ocean's attitude to the everyday is echoed in his approach to colour, which he is aware that many people might think drab. To him, however, it is far from that – it is 'the colour that I see and I don't want to heighten it in any way – it's wonderful enough as it is, and if it's not wonderful I might as well roll over and go back to sleep.'

Tangerine Static, 2012
Oil on canvas
102 × 127 cm

Hughie O'Donoghue RA

Born: 5 July 1953, Manchester, UK
Elected RA: 28 May 2009
Category of Membership: Painter

Hughie O'Donoghue graduated from Goldsmiths College, London, in 1982 and has since exhibited regularly and widely across Europe and America. Recent solo exhibitions include Marlborough Fine Art (2012), DOX Centre for Contemporary Art, Prague (2011) and Michael Janssen Gallery, Berlin (2007). After leaving art school in the firm knowledge that he, unlike many of his peers, did not want to be a conceptual artist, he found himself drawn to the images of recently excavated Iron Age remains. They inspired a series of carefully researched and hauntingly executed 'Sleeper' paintings, qualities that have remained characteristic of O'Donoghue's work.

The artist is fascinated with the anonymous individual; engaging with the past, his expressive paintings use mythology, history and personal records to explore human experience. *Talisman* has as its subject a fragment of a stone sculpture of a garlanded human head, which O'Donoghue has situated within a windswept landscape. The model for the painting was the fragment embedded in the wall of the graphic studio in Venice where he worked last summer. A representation of the Green Man, it was believed to have originated in Constantinople and brought back to Venice as a trophy from a voyage overseas.

Such fragments have been a recurrent motif in O'Donoghue's work: the association of stone with antiquity compels him, for the fact that it was one of the earliest ways to record history as much as for its durability. *Talisman* synthesises this notion with the story of a sculpture that – according to the oral history of the Inishkea Islands off the coast of North West Mayo – was regarded as a protective, benign presence by the islanders: a lucky talisman. A visiting cleric, believing it to be an idol, took exception to it and ordered it to be thrown into the sea. In 1927 a violent storm killed the majority of the male population who were fishing at the time, and the islands have been uninhabited ever since.

Talisman, 2010/12
Oil on linen canvas
71 × 106 cm

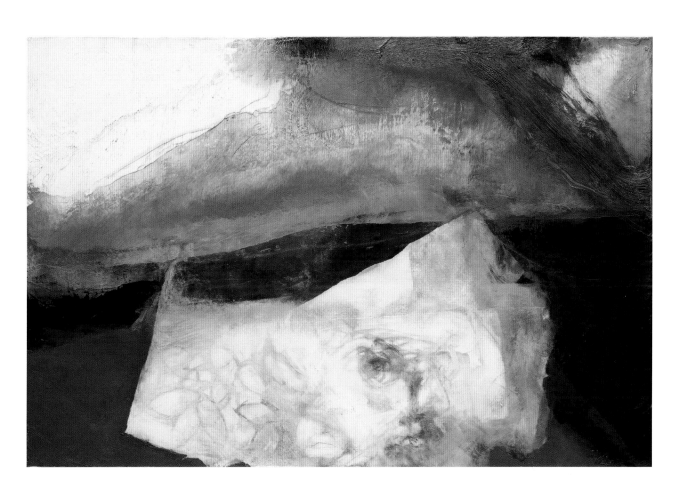

Chris Orr RA

Born: 8 April 1943, London, UK
Elected RA: 22 May 1995
Category of Membership: Engraver

Chris Orr studied at Ravensbourne College of Art, Hornsey College of Art and the Royal College of Art, London. Throughout his career as a painter-printmaker he has held teaching posts at Cardiff College of Art, St Martin's School of Art and Design, and the Royal College of Art where on finishing as Professor of Printmaking in 1998 Orr was made Professor Emeritus. He has exhibited extensively worldwide including Tokyo, New York and Australia, as well as holding regular exhibitions at the Jill George Gallery, London, since 1978.

Although often awarded the title of a modern-day Hogarth, the world that Orr creates in his rich and detailed images doesn't have the intense didactic preaching of his eighteenth-century predecessor, and instead brims with a fantastical and, at times, eccentric set of characters and locations. As Fiona Maddocks wrote of his teeming images: 'To see one is to enter a world of glorious human chaos, with Orr the grand puppeteer, pulling strings to impose his own kind of order.'

Orr says: 'In the past few years I have begun to produce work about cities that tries to deal with both how things appear and what lies beneath that appearance.' This particular work references the famous seventeenth-century etcher Wenceslaus Hollar, who lived and worked in London and captured the city on the verge of change, with Civil War, social unrest, an influx of people from across Europe and widening social divides, all thrown together in the close-knit metropolis. In Orr's print we are met with Harlequins, knights, bear-baiters and prostitutes, cast alongside a menagerie of animals and set within a dense landscape of higgledy-piggledy buildings, church spires, theatres and mills. Orr presents a meticulous mosaic of this fictionalised London life, whose everyday disorder and chaos is still so easily recognisable today.

On the Road to Damascus, a London Fantasy based on Wenceslaus Hollar and Others, 2012
Hand-coloured drypoint
71 × 104 cm

Mimmo Paladino Hon RA

Born: 18 December 1948, Paduli, Campania, southern Italy
Elected Honorary RA: 26 May 1999

Mimmo Paladino is an Italian sculptor, painter and printmaker. Despite attending the Liceo Artistico di Benevento (1964–8) when minimalism and conceptualism dominated the international art scene, he is associated with the revival of painting in the late 1970s. His work has been shown in many prestigious group exhibitions worldwide including the Paris, Venice and Sydney biennales and the Royal Academy's seminal 1981 exhibition 'A New Spirit in Painting'. He has had numerous solo shows that include Forte Belvedere, Florence (1993), South London Gallery (1999), Centro per l'Arte Contemporanea Luigi Pecci, Prato, Italy (2002–03) and the Estorick Collection, London (2004). His work is held in major public collections worldwide including The Museum of Modern Art and the Solomon R. Guggenheim Museum, New York, Tate, the Kunstmuseum, Basel, and the Nationalgalerie, Berlin. He has also designed several theatre sets, and collaborated with musician Brian Eno on two occasions: at the Roundhouse,

London (1999) and Museo dell'Ara Pacis, Rome (2008). He lives and works in Rome, Paduli and Puglia in Italy.

Paladino insists that his art is nomadic, 'crossing the various territories of art, both in a geographical and a temporal sense, and with maximum technical and creative freedom'. Certainly the motifs that dominate his work transcend boundaries by appealing to a shared humanity. Disembodied heads, like the two that turn away from us in this work, feature regularly in his work. Symmetry, posture and the dominance of the central, abstract white form combine to create a sense of mystery and isolation. Paladino has prevented the most emotive of imagery – the human face – from providing any narrative; instead, we are left only with our sensations. The symbolic use of figuration speaks of his belief that 'art is not a superficial thing, nor a sociological thing, nor a poetic storm. Art is a slow process around a language of signs.'

Untitled, 1998
Mixed media on canvas
46 × 65 cm

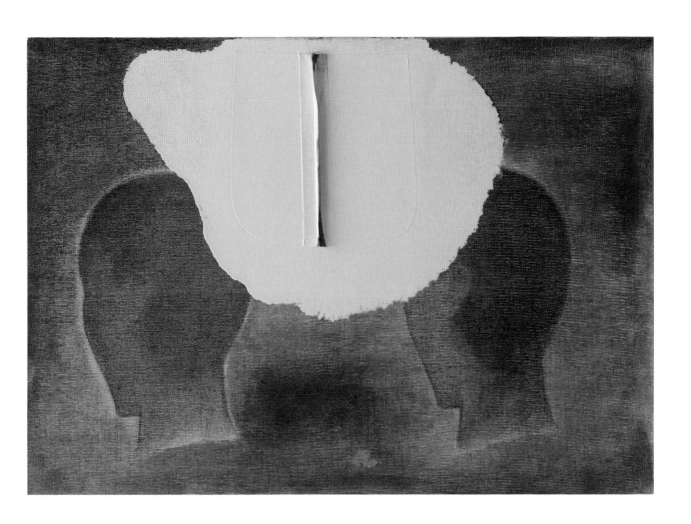

Cornelia Parker RA

Born: 14 July 1956, Cheshire, UK
Elected RA: 8 December 2009
Category of Membership: Sculptor

Cornelia Parker studied at Gloucester College of Art, Wolverhampton Polytechnic and Reading University. In 1997 she was shortlisted for the Turner Prize. Examples of her work include the suspended elements of an exploded shed entitled *Cold Dark Matter: An Exploded View* (1991), *The Maybe* (1995), a collaborative piece with Tilda Swinton, and *Anti-Mass* (2005), a sculpture composed from the charred remains of a church destroyed by arson. Parker has had solo exhibitions in England, Europe and both North and South America, including the Serpentine Gallery, London (1998), ICA Boston (2000), the Kunstverein in Stuttgart (2004) and the Museo de Arte de Lima in Peru (2008). She was awarded an OBE in 2010.

'I resurrect things that have been killed off…

My work is all about the potential of materials – even when it looks like they've lost all possibilities.' Parker's sculptures are often site-specific installations composed of found objects and materials, which question the nature of matter and its possibility of transformation. *Poison and Antidote Drawing* was made using rattlesnake venom in a suspension of black ink, with its antidote present within the white ink. The result is a work laced both with the destructive and the restorative. The interrelation between these two polar elements within a shape akin to a Rorschach test suggests the close relationship between life and death, destruction and salvation, matter and immateriality, and implies the part that the mind plays in animating such elements, transcending their material existence.

Poison and Antidote Drawing, 2010
Rattlesnake venom and black ink,
anti-venom and white ink
37 × 37 cm

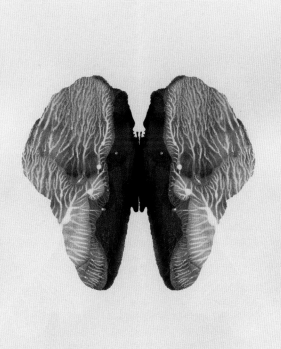

Eric Parry RA

Born: 24 March 1952, Kuwait City
Elected RA: 12 December 2006
Category of Membership: Architect

Eric Parry studied architecture at the University of Newcastle, the Royal College of Art and the Architectural Association. He founded his practice in 1983, the same year that he was appointed as a lecturer in architecture at the University of Cambridge, a post he held until 1997. He has also lectured at the Graduate School of Design, Harvard University, the University of Houston and the Tokyo Institute of Technology. Early projects include student accommodation for Pembroke College, Cambridge, and luxury apartments in Kuala Lumpur. In 2003 an innovative office development at 30 Finsbury Square won a RIBA Regional award and was shortlisted for the RIBA Stirling Prize for Architecture, as was the City office building 5 Aldermanbury Square in 2009. More recent projects include the redevelopment of 50 New Bond Street and 14 St George Street, London, the regeneration of St Martin-in-the-Fields, and the Holburne Museum, Bath. Parry was President of the Architectural Association (2005–07) and currently serves on the Kettle's Yard Committee and the Mayor's Design Advisory Panel.

'I've drawn ever since I can remember – just pencil on paper. It's a process of discovery, both for work and pleasure.' Although Parry is known for his architecture, he has also studied and practised art. In the mid-1970s he took time off from his architecture studies to travel and to pursue his passion for art. He embarked on a foundation course at Hornsey School of Art, following this with two years at the Royal College of Art. In this painting one can sense the interplay between Parry's two disciplines. It is a vibrant display of dynamic shape and undulating sculptural form, evoking vital energy. Beneath the bright colours and curved accents, however, straight lines, geometric shapes, neutral tones and divisions suggest that aesthetic interest develops from structured foundations.

Natura 1, 2010
Acrylic on watercolour paper
51 × 172 cm

John Partridge RA

Born: 26 August 1924, London, UK
Elected ARA: 21 May 1980
Elected RA: 8 December 1988
Category of Membership: Architect

John Partridge executed this elegant drawing of The Queen's House on the river in Greenwich, designed by Inigo Jones in the early seventeenth century, while he was still a student at the Regent Street Polytechnic. It was a period when the debate between the forces of modernism and traditionalism in architecture was at its height. Upon graduating in 1951 he worked for what was at the time the largest architects' office in the world, within the London County Council. By the latter half of the decade the focus of stylistic disagreement had shifted. The modernist movement had fractured into two camps: those that favoured design based on Marxist principles, and those who believed in the currency and utility of Le Corbusier's modernist precepts.

In 1959 Partridge and three ideologically sympathetic colleagues set up the Howell Killick Partridge & Amis (HKPA) practice that espoused the latter principles. They believed in the validity of an analytical approach to building design, and aimed to develop a richer language from the basic vocabulary of geometry and movement structures that had already been established. Partridge's work with this practice encompassed many university projects, such as St Antony's and the Reyne and Wolfson Buildings, St Anne's College, Oxford University. He approached such schemes as a collection of individual living units, rather than starting with the idea of the building as a monolithic block. This enabled each element to be pre-cast and then amalgamated into powerful, almost sculptural forms that speak strongly of their internal structure and construction. Although concrete fell out of fashion and Partridge began to use other materials, he continued to conceive his designs in this constructivist manner, working on a wide range of buildings such as the Hall of Justice for Trinidad and Tobago, and Chaucer College at the University of Kent. This early sketch already demonstrates Partridge's draughtsman skills.

The Queen's House, Greenwich, 1947
Pencil drawing on cartridge paper
61 × 81 cm

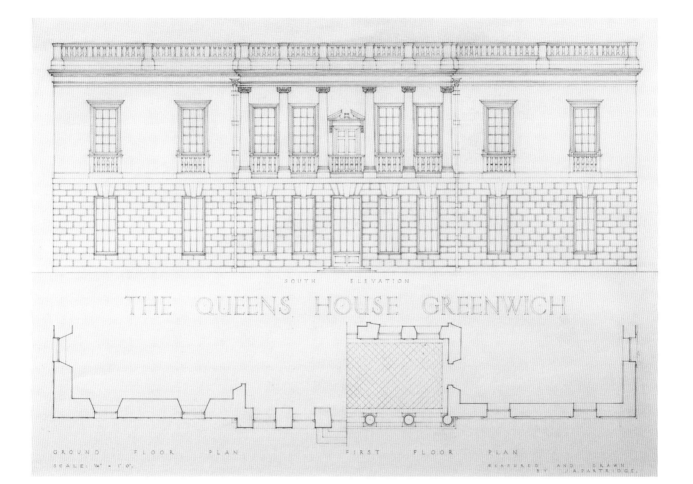

SOUTH ELEVATION

THE QUEENS HOUSE GREENWICH

GROUND FLOOR PLAN

FIRST FLOOR PLAN

SCALE: ¼" = 1'0".

MEASURED AND DRAWN
BY J.A.PARTRIDGE.

Grayson Perry RA

Born: 24 March 1960, Chelmsford, Essex, UK
Elected RA: 15 March 2011
Category of Membership: Printmaker

Grayson Perry describes himself as a craftsman in an art world that he feels often eschews craft in favour of concept. He is unashamed of many things: his background – he grew up in Essex in what he has described as a 'dysfunctional family' and studied at the Braintree College and Portsmouth Polytechnic – and his transvestism. When Perry was awarded the Turner Prize in 2003 he dressed as his alter-ego, Claire, making his acceptance perhaps the most memorable in the prize's long history.

Perry works across a variety of mediums, but is particularly well known for his work as a ceramicist, and latterly for his tapestry works. Uniting the work is an honest fascination with human psychology and a mischievous interest in the relationship between the subject and the objects' form. Ceramics appeal to Perry because they haven't got 'any big pretensions to being great public works of art, and no matter

how brash a statement I make, on a pot it will always have certain humility'.

This specially created, colourfully illustrated pot has been made in the tradition of historical portraits of Royal Academicians, and is both a comment on Perry's experience of being an RA as well as an affectionate satire of its assorted members. He is as yet undecided about providing a key to identify the numbered figures as they should perhaps be seen more as a scheme of decoration rather than formal portraits. 'In the art world,' he says, 'decorativeness is a quality often referred to pejoratively. I see decorativeness as one of the most noble and skilful attributes of any artwork. I wanted this pot to be quite jolly as that is my experience so far of being an RA, lots of fun drinking. Jolliness and decorativeness – what more can we ask of the establishment?'

Bad Portraits of Establishment Figures I (preparatory sketch), 2012
Ceramic pot
Height 78 cm

Tom Phillips RA

Born: 24 May 1937, London, UK
Elected ARA: 9 May 1984
Elected RA: 7 December 1989
Category of Membership: Printmaker

Tom Phillips read English at St Catherine's College, Oxford, in 1957 while simultaneously studied drawing at the Ruskin School. Between 1961 and 1963 he attended Camberwell School of Art under the tutelage of Frank Auerbach. He went on to teach at Bath Academy of Art, Ipswich, and Wolverhampton Art College. Since his first solo show at the Artists International Association Gallery in 1965 he has gone on to exhibit in a number of solo and group exhibitions worldwide, most significantly at the Kunsthalle, Basel, the National Portrait Gallery, London, the Modern Art Museum in Fort Worth, USA, and the Royal Academy of Arts where he chaired the Academy's library and exhibition committees between 1995 and 2007.

Phillips generates multi-layered images that are both decorative and sensual in equal measure. Language plays a central role in his work, as demonstrated by his seminal visual-poetic artist's book

A Humument. The disparate styles and themes that appear side-by-side within Phillips' body of work have been said 'to bring about a sense of cacophony or awe'; but, when his oeuvre is further explored 'each of these styles and themes can be demonstrated to have a long-standing lineage in time'.

Quantum Poetics Chapter I started life as the study for a portrait upon which Phillips improvised freely. 'Without any plan, shapes emerged like clouds forming and reforming. Each layer of the painting revealed the layers beneath in the form of dots or patterns or larger areas where I liked and left the accidents of colours already present; in effect an abstract palimpsest.' Phillips describes how the dark shapes within the work 'have resolved themselves into a kind of cloud calligraphy, which suggests a desire to expand into a larger area'.

Quantum Poetics Chapter I, 2010
Epson and silkscreen (edition of 25)
167.5 × 52 cm

Barbara Rae RA

Born: 10 December 1943, Falkirk, Stirlingshire, Scotland, UK
Elected RA: 29 May 1996
Category of Membership: Painter and Printmaker

Barbara Rae studied at Edinburgh College of Art, where she was awarded a travel scholarship that took her to work in France and Spain in 1966. Her first solo show was held in 1967 at the New 57 Gallery, Edinburgh, and she has exhibited internationally since. She has won numerous prestigious awards and her work is in private, public and commercial collections worldwide. She has also completed tapestry commissions for the Festival Theatre and the Royal Scottish Museum in Edinburgh.

Rae is celebrated for her vivid work inspired by aspects in landscapes that have been crafted, created or altered by the hand of man. Their exuberance issues from a distinct genius with colour and her technique of applying pigments directly onto the canvas and pouring fluid over them so that they mix and blend.

She travels widely and often, absorbing herself in the history of a location by walking, drawing and photographing it. 'When I'm working on an exhibition, I shoot off to different places. I research each study carefully,' she says. 'I'm not interested in topographical detail. I immerse myself in the culture of a place.' This includes time spent looking at the sacred symbols of the indigenous ancient peoples, which she then incorporates into her images to get a sense of their spiritual world. Once back in her studio, she uses the studies as 'the beginning, the formal structure – the drawings are the starting point for something I play around with'. The resulting work is dynamic and alive, capturing the immediacy of the place, but above all it conveys a sense of the people that lived there.

Andalusia, 2009
Mixed media on canvas
209 × 234 cm

Fiona Rae RA

Born: 10 October 1963, Hong Kong
Elected RA: 28 May 2002
Category of Membership: Painter

Fiona Rae studied at Croydon College of Art and Goldsmiths College of Art, and within four years of graduating she had been nominated for the Turner Prize. Part of the generation who became known as YBAs (Young British Artists), her work has been included in seminal group shows including 'Freeze' (1988), 'Sensation' at the Royal Academy of Arts (1997), 'Fiction@Love' at Shanghai Museum of Contemporary Art and Singapore Art Museum (2006) and 'Classified: Contemporary Art at Tate Britain' (2009). She has held major solo exhibitions at Kunsthalle Basel, Switzerland (1992), Institute of Contemporary Arts, London (1993/4), Carré d'Art – Musée d'Art Contemporain, Nîmes (2002), Leeds Art Gallery (2012) and The New Art Gallery Walsall (2012). Her work is featured in numerous prestigious private and public collections worldwide.

Rae has created a highly personal invented world within which her marks, gestures and imagery debate a new synthesis of painterly languages and challenge the modern conventions of painting. She has explored collage in her works on paper throughout the last decade, finely tuned compositions that reflect the artist's flair for surprising juxtapositions and expressive freedom. Rae includes a profusion of contrasting materials: abstract brush marks are confronted by the geometric artifice of overlain black lace; cartoon animals are threatened by enveloping pools of acrylic paint; butterflies and birds dance triumphantly about the surface, echoed by neat black silk bows. The composition is balanced yet fragile. Although there is great ebullience in the bricolage, one can also detect an underlying, unsettling dialogue. Rae says she is constantly 'asking what would take it further, what would challenge it in an interesting way?' Incorporating the pretty, the sinister, the playful and the sombre, her work questions the choice of imagery in art – the tensions between what is considered meaningful, what is dismissed as decorative and why.

Untitled (Orange with Black Lace), 2009
Mixed media on archive paper
59.4 × 41.9 cm

David Remfry RA

Born: 30 July 1942, Worthing, Sussex, UK
Elected RA: 2 June 2006
Category of Membership: Painter

David Remfry studied at Hull College of Art. His first solo show was in London in 1973, and since then he has had over 50 solo shows across the world and in various museums, including the National Portrait Gallery and the Victoria and Albert Museum, London, and Museum of Modern Art / PS1, New York. He was made a member of the Royal Watercolour Society in 1987, received an MBE for services to British Art in America in 2001, received an Honorary Doctorate of Arts from the University of Lincoln in 2007 and won the Hugh Casson Drawing Prize at the Royal Academy's 'Summer Exhibition' in 2010.

Remfry is perhaps best known for his works in watercolour. He defies tradition by painting large figures in motion – sometimes nearing life-sized – often dancers, one of his most visited subjects. This work is in many ways typical of Remfry. He depicts people very sensually, and is known for an urban style that *Lulu* encapsulates perfectly. Her hair and her mouth have been accentuated with thick, dark graphite strokes drawing the viewer's eye first to her face. It is drawn with no tone other than the woman's glasses, creating a contrast between the dark hair and lips and the smooth white skin. The concealed eyes make the figure more elusive, and a tattoo of a cat on the woman's arm draws the eye down. Remfry's confident use of line creates movement, and as she seemingly walks away from us we are drawn into the picture, intrigued to follow.

Remfry prefers not to use professional models, but people who possess some quality that suits his work. He finds New York, where he moved in 1995, rich in subject-matter. He saw Lulu walking on 7th Avenue in her customary black, and she agreed to sit for him. He regards the work as significant in that the model was the first he worked with in New York, and this is the first of numerous drawings and paintings in which she appears.

Lulu, 1995
Graphite on paper
66 × 56 cm

Ian Ritchie RA

Born: 24 June 1947, Hove, Sussex, UK
Elected RA: 10 December 1998
Elected RA Professor of Architecture: December 2004
Category of Membership: Architect

Founded in 1981, Ian Ritchie Architects has achieved international acclaim, winning more than 60 awards including the Iritecna Prize for Europe, the Commonwealth Association of Architects Award for the Advancement of Architecture as well as being shortlisted for the RIBA Stirling Prize four times. It has worked on many landmark projects throughout Europe including the Reina Sofia Museum of Modern Art, Madrid, and the Royal Shakespeare Company Courtyard Theatre, Stratford-upon-Avon. Ian Ritchie has devoted much time to teaching and lecturing; he was the Visiting Professor at Leeds University School of Civil Engineering (2001–04), has lectured at TU Vienna, Moscow and Liverpool Universities and has also taught at the Architectural Association. In 2000 he was awarded the French Academie d'Architecture Grand Silver Medal for Innovation as well as a CBE.

Ritchie writes poetry at the start of a commission to understand the nuances and specific requirements particular to each site and project; using language he brings his ideas into focus. Once understanding the interrelation of word and form, he distils these ideas into delicate etchings and drawings that form the beginning of his designs. 'The drawing', Ritchie says, 'attempts to synthesise and reveal the essential aspects derived from my investigative writing. The paper is changed from white emptiness forever, from white light to black line, even black light.'

This sensitivity is reflected in the uniquely broad view that Ritchie takes when approaching a project, and his architectural practice establishes a clear idea of a site's aesthetic, social and ecological values as well as its spatial and physical aspects. The firm's winning designs include the Alba di Milano, France-Japan Monument, The Spire of Dublin and the Pearl of Dubai; their nascent forms can be seen here as etchings. Although technologically innovative, it is the fundamental understanding at the root of all Ritchie's realised projects that allows them to suit past, present and future contexts.

Etchings: *Alba di Milano,* 2000, 26 × 26 cm; *British Museum Study,* 2006, 28 × 38 cm *France-Japan Monument,* 2005, 19 × 37 cm; *Freedom and Unity Memorial, Berlin,* 2011, 34 × 44 cm (pair); *Landmark Wales,* 2010, 28 × 33 cm; *Monument for Ireland (white),* 2003, 39 × 14 cm; *Monument for Ireland,* 1999, 39 × 14 cm; *Pearl of Dubai – fine series,* 2008, 33.5 × 25.5 cm

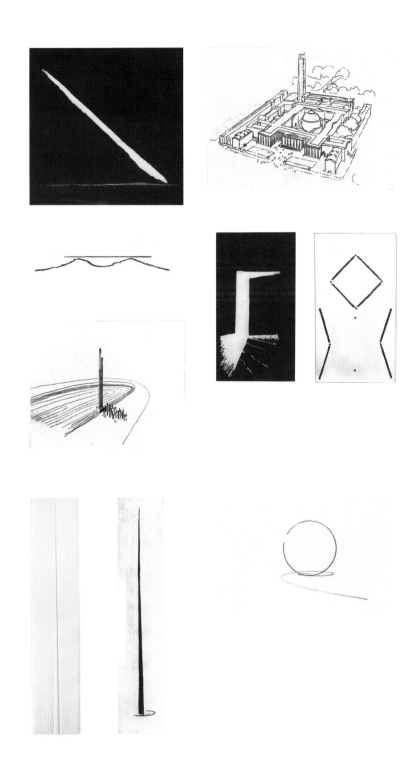

Richard Rogers RA

Born: 23 July 1933, Florence, Italy
Elected ARA: 11 May 1978
Elected RA: 9 May 1984
Category of Membership: Architect

Richard Rogers studied at the Architectural Association and Yale before founding Team 4 with Norman Foster, and later the Design Research unit with Renzo Piano. Winning the commission to design the Pompidou Centre, Paris, in 1971 transformed his reputation and practice. Embodying the youthful spirit of the late 1960s, Rogers and Piano aimed to create a meaningful, egalitarian public space for all. This commitment to produce work that benefits society is still at the heart of the Rogers' design practice. Over the last three decades Rogers Stirk Harbour + Partners has attracted some of architecture's most prestigious commissions, awards and critical acclaim. Designing a wide range of building types across the globe, including Terminal 4 at Madrid-Barajas Airport and Maggie's Centre, London (both of which received RIBA Stirling prizes), Rogers continues to spearhead innovative and quality architecture.

Set amidst the treetops of the Chateau La Coste estate, this sketch shows Rogers' design for a new gallery space and viewing platform that will project dramatically out over the Provence landscape. The 225 m² pavilion has been designed to house small works of art with a roof terrace/sculpture garden. Visitors can access the terrace directly from a nearby ridge walk and so the entire building becomes an extension of the terrain, providing stunning views of the surrounding vineyards. The gallery is essentially one large cantilever, held on to the hillside by a concrete anchor. A steel frame comprising a series of brightly coloured trusses allows the entire building to protrude out of the hill. Diagonal tension cables provide additional support for each truss and delicately animate the façade.

This pavilion is one of many that have been bought or commissioned from some of the biggest names in international architecture. With a winery designed by Jean Nouvel and pavilions from Frank Gehry and Toyo Ito, this estate will become a destination for both wine lovers and lovers of design.

Chateau La Coste Gallery, 2012
Concept sketch: ink on paper
21 × 29.7 cm

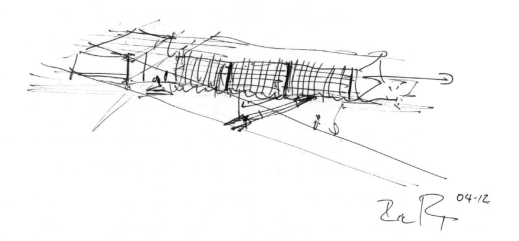

04-12

Mick Rooney RA

Born: 5 March 1944, Epsom, Surrey, UK
Elected ARA: 31 May 1990
Elected RA: 26 June 1991
Category of Membership: Painter

Mick Rooney studied at Sutton School of Art, Wimbledon School of Art and the Royal College of Art, London, after which he was awarded the Austin Abbey Major Scholarship to study at the British School at Rome for four years. He has exhibited throughout Britain and Europe and held various teaching posts in colleges across the country, including Head of Painting at the Royal Academy Schools (1991–6). Rooney has received numerous prizes and commissions, including the Korn/Ferry International Premier Award at the Royal Academy's 'Summer Exhibition' in 1989. In 1992 he was commissioned by Transport for London to design a poster to advertise the Brick Lane Clothes Show, which ran throughout the London Underground. His work is in many public collections throughout the world including the Gulbenkian

Foundation and the Jerwood Foundation.

Having travelled extensively in Europe, North Africa and Mexico, Rooney is drawn towards a predominantly figurative tradition that focuses on the narrative of the scene before him. His bold, rounded and familiar characters carry a surrealist edge that is executed with the warmth and charm of a true observer of human behaviour. Viewers can easily relate to Rooney's paintings, whether it is the fairy-tale scenes of Spanish matadors and flamenco dancers, or his more personalised depictions of characters going about their everyday lives. There is a warmth and familiarity in this picture that is found in much of Rooney's work: in the soft Mediterranean glow we see five cyclists caught by the artist at a moment of rest in the midst of a rural landscape that is both tranquil and unhurried.

Peloton Before a Shrine, 2011
Oil on canvas
60.9 × 91.4 cm

Ed Ruscha Hon RA

Born: 16 December 1937, Omaha, Nebraska, USA
Elected Honorary RA: 26 May 2004

Ed Ruscha was born in Omaha, Nebraska, and raised in Oklahoma City, Oklahoma, USA. In 1956 he moved to Los Angeles where he studied painting, photography and graphic design at the Chouinard Art Institute. He had his first solo exhibition in 1963 at the Ferus Gallery in Los Angeles. His earliest international retrospective was in 1982 at the San Francisco Museum of Modern Art, and the Hayward Gallery, London, hosted his most recent in 2009. He currently shows with Gagosian Gallery and continues to live and work in Los Angeles.

Ruscha acknowledges that his work has been a variation on a theme that began when he first moved to LA. He started out as a commercial artist, something that continues to exert a strong influence on his artistic oeuvre. Rebelling in part against the spontaneous nature of abstract expressionism, he found that preconceiving an image was 'a delicious approach to making a picture'. Whether in

beautifully produced artist's books, painting, drawing or photography, Ruscha has consistently combined realistic imagery of the world around him with vernacular language and bold text to communicate a particular urban experience.

The words that Ruscha picks to hover in front of an image, however, come to him more organically, and are often picked simply because of the beauty of the letterforms. It is this and the interplay of word and image that awakens our curiosity. The letters UNGKAY are as ambiguous as the monochrome image over which they are suspended, and they hold our attention while we try to discern an association. The background is reminiscent of stormy skies, rain-splattered surfaces and shadows formed by clouds, but equally the darker periphery and pattern could represent urban ubiquity: the illumination of a car's headlight on a road, a dirt-strewn wall. 'Art has to be something that makes you scratch your head,' says Ruscha.

UNGKAY, 2008
Acrylic on museum board paper
35.6 × 50.8 cm

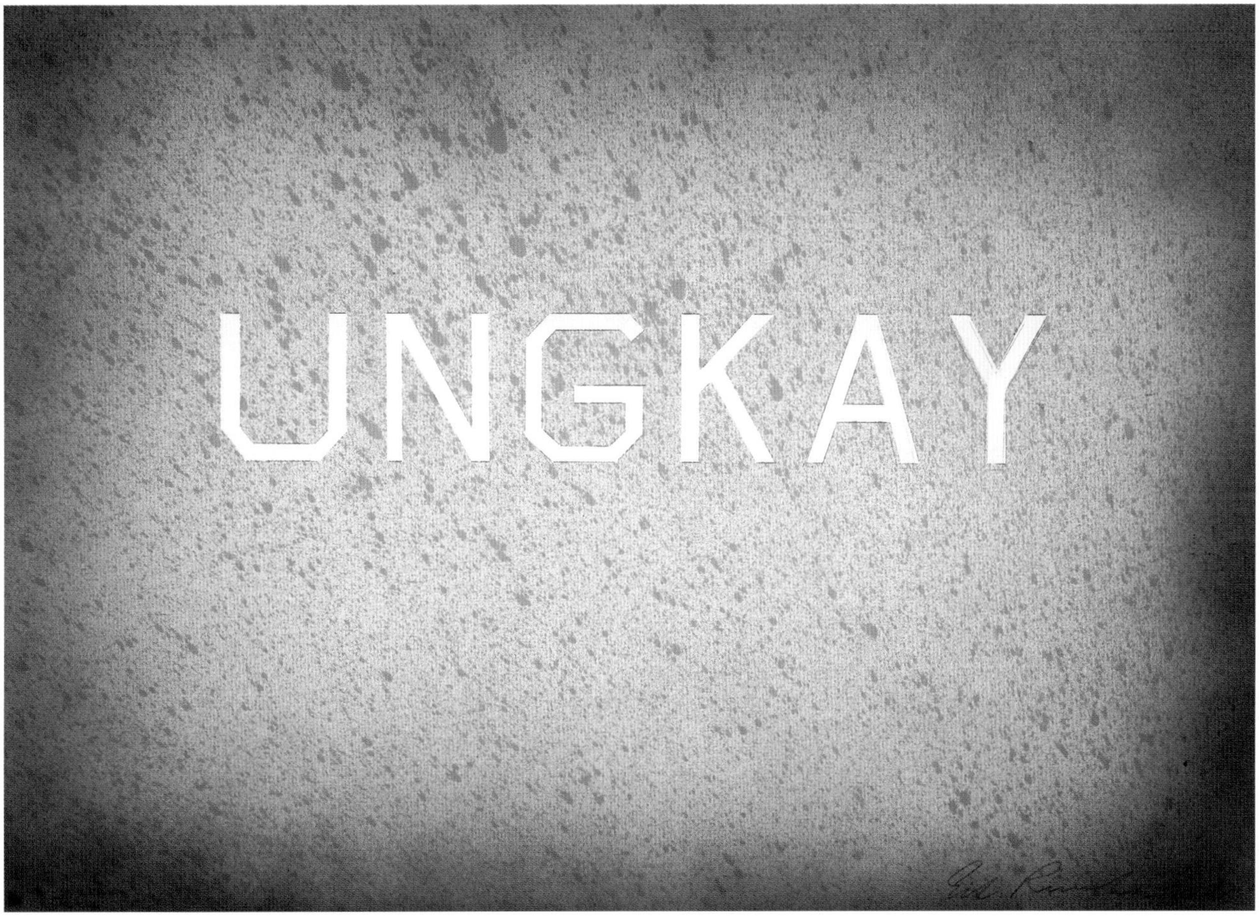
UNGKAY

Michael Sandle RA

Born: 18 May 1936, Weymouth, Dorset, UK
Re-elected RA: 26 May 2004
Category of Membership: Sculptor

Michael Sandle studied at Douglas School of
Art and Technology on the Isle of Man before
completing his studies at the Slade School of Fine
Art, London, in 1959. He then moved to Paris for a
year to concentrate on lithography. Working in a broad
variety of mediums, Sandle has held teaching posts
throughout Britain as well as in Canada and, from the
late 1970s, in Germany. He held his first solo exhibition
at Drian Gallery, London, in 1963, and has since
exhibited regularly in Britain and abroad, including an
important retrospective of his work at the Whitechapel
Gallery in 1988.

Attracted to themes of warfare and mortality,
Sandle is perhaps best known for his large-scale
commissioned sculptures, such as *St George and the
Dragon* in Blackfriars, London (1988), that serve to
emphasise the craftsmanship inherent in his workings.
Frequently deploying myth and legend as a means of
communicating ideas, he uses drawings to explore
certain motifs before committing them to sculpture, as
seen in this work. Here, Sandle looks to the eleventh-
century ruler of Dublin and King of Mann and the
Isles, Godred Crovan. Displaying the ruler in a typically
heroic stance with bold, angular lines in both the
figure and the head of the horse, it is an excellent
example of Sandle's skill as a draughtsman. There is
an overriding sense of nostalgia both in the subject-
matter and in the somewhat subdued palette, which
the artist uses to imbue the work with a delicacy and
romanticised charm.

Godred Crovan – Variation II, 2004
Watercolour
153 × 93 cm

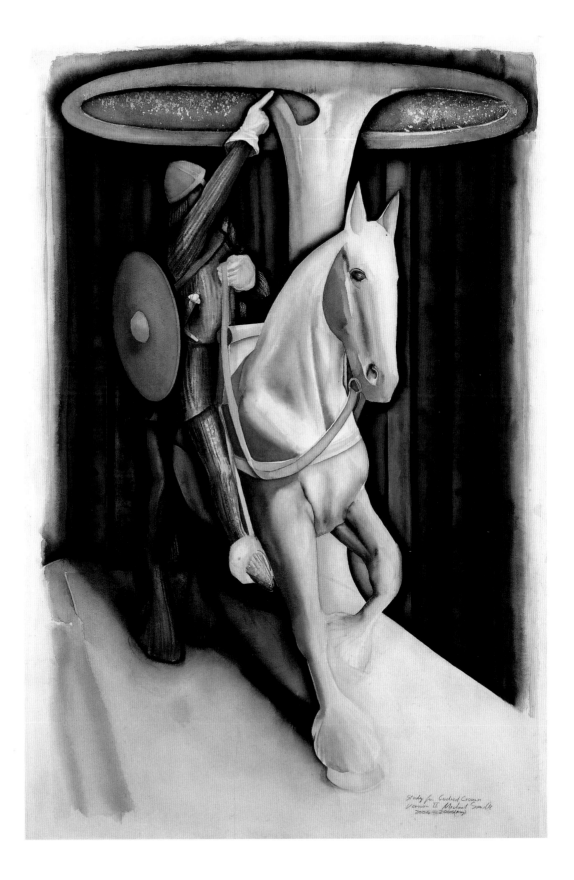

Study for Crooked Crown
Version II Michael Smith
2004–2006 (ong)

Jenny Saville RA

Born: 7 May 1970, Cambridge, UK
Elected RA: 31 May 2007
Category of Membership: Painter

An alumnus of Glasgow School of Art and lecturer at the Slade School of Fine Arts between 2000 and 2006, Jenny Saville has become renowned for her large-scale oil paintings of obese female figures, including the famous work *Plan* (1983) in which a naked woman is pictured, almost cartographically, from above. So synonymous has she become with this Rubenesque vision of the female body that critics and collectors are often surprised to find that Saville herself cuts a rather diminutive figure.

The Palermo-based artist has exhibited in numerous important group shows including 'Young British Artists III' at the Saatchi Gallery (1994) and the iconic 'Sensation' show at the Royal Academy (1997). Major solo shows followed at the New York Gagosian Gallery – 'Territories' in 1999 and 'Migrants' in 2003.

In 2005 Saville was the subject of an in-depth survey exhibition at the Museo d'Arte Contemporanea in Rome, and the influential collector Carlo Bilotti commissioned three artworks for the inaugural exhibition of Rome's Museo Carlo Bilotti in 2006.

Saville's canvases are extravagant in every sense: in scale, in the abundant bodies of their subjects and in the liberal use of paint. Her subjects are not drawn from life, but are 'discovered' – in photographs, medical textbooks and newspapers. Saville has even attended plastic surgery operations in the name of fleshly research.

This study disrupts the conventional beauty of the classical mother and child scene, with the dual sense of attraction and repulsion common to Saville's work.

Mother and Child Study II, 2009
Pencil on vellum
90.5 × 59.5 cm

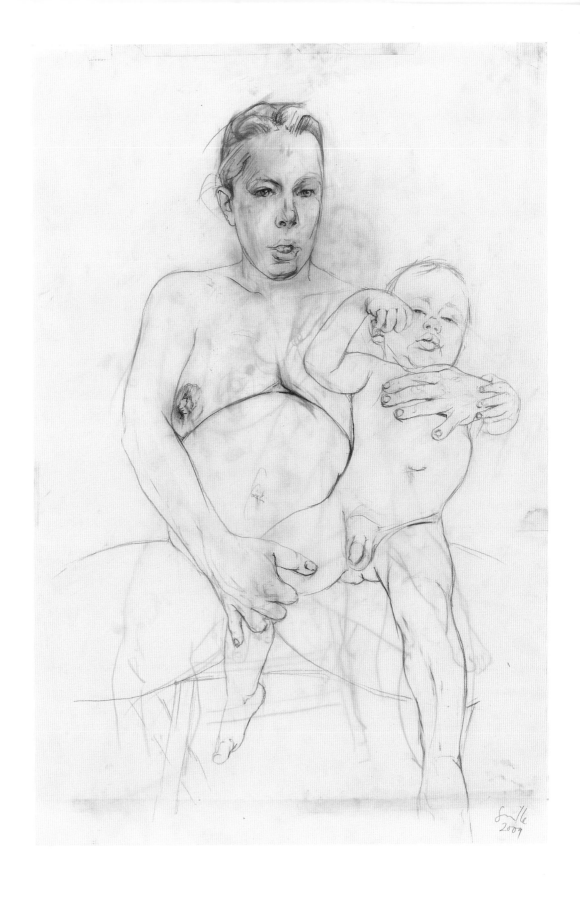

Terry Setch RA

Born: 11 March 1936, Lewisham, London, UK
Elected RA: 28 May 2009
Category of Membership: Painter

Terry Setch studied at Sutton and Cheam School of Art before moving on to the Slade School of Fine Art. His paintings have been widely exhibited in the UK and abroad and he has received numerous prizes and awards. He is represented in permanent collections including Tate, the Arts Council, British Council, Victoria and Albert Museum, London, National Museum of Wales and other public collections across the UK and abroad.

Setch moved to Wales in 1964 and draws much of his inspiration from his surroundings, mainly focusing on a particular two-mile stretch of beach between Penarth and Lavernock Point. His landscape-based paintings celebrate the natural beauty of the beach and headland, while simultaneously commenting on the challenges to the natural world that have been posed by global environmental issues.

Setch's works attempt to symbolise a sense of place rather than providing literal representations. *Lavernock Shore* is a personal and intuitive response to his long acquaintance with the landscape. Setch has said that his paintings 'engage with the sensation of being in a sharp terrain of ancient geology, of clambering over rocks and becoming so familiar with the surroundings that you can interpret from where water breaks or in the shifts and ridges between land and island how this place has altered and persisted over millions of years'.

Through his instinctive touch Setch is able to bring forth the sense of change, flux, fusion and growth experienced on the shore at Lavernock Point. 'It can be violent and frightening there,' he says. 'I attempt to bring that restlessness, that urgency to make new things on the foundations of the old, into my painting.'

Lavernock Shore, 2010
Encaustic wax and pigment on board
24 × 43 cm

Cindy Sherman Hon RA

Born: 19 January 1954, Glen Ridge, New Jersey, USA
Elected Honorary RA: 16 March 2010

Cindy Sherman's explosive work has made a definitive contribution to the post-modern conversation around women, the media and the broader nature of art.

Born in New Jersey, Sherman discovered a love for the visual arts while at Buffalo State College, and which quickly developed into a particular fascination with photography. She began documenting the process of transformation through dress and make-up, a theme that has run through her work to the present day. This process of altering physique and surroundings has enabled her to explore the concept of contemporary identity in a deft, eloquent and provocative way. Her work has been shown extensively around the world, including in the Venice Biennale, five Whitney Biennials and the world's leading galleries and exhibition spaces. In 2012 New York's Museum of Modern Art mounted a major solo retrospective that is due to travel to the San Francisco Museum of Modern Art and the Walker Art Center in Minneapolis.

Sherman shoots her work, most often in series, alone in her studio, playfully assuming the multiple technical roles alongside the photographer – director, make-up artist, stylist, hairdresser and model of multiple personae. Her enjoyment of this process emanates from the final work. Here, as in much of her work, there is a sexual frisson in her adoption of both the male and female characters – the direct, swaggering male doctor and the coy female nurse. Sherman makes a point about rigid gender roles, but she does so with humour and a talent for character-play that means her work is always enjoyable before it is instructive.

Untitled, 1980/2000
Two sepia tone photographs
25.4 × 20.3 cm each

Alan Stanton RA

Born: 19 April 1944, Northampton, UK
Elected RA: 8 December 2009
Category of Membership: Architect

Alan Stanton studied at the Architectural Association in London and worked with Norman Foster for a brief period before relocating to California, where he studied at UCLA and was awarded a fellowship in Urban Design. Returning to Europe, he collaborated with Renzo Piano and Richard Rogers on the Pompidou Centre in Paris, after which he taught at the Architectural Association. In 1985 he and Paul Williams established their practice, Stanton Williams. Notable projects include Compton Verney Art Gallery, Warwickshire, the Millennium Seed Bank at Wakehurst Place, West Sussex, and Tower Hill Square at the Tower of London.

Stanton Williams has a distinctive architectural vision that is anchored by its aesthetic belief in the importance of space as a condition for great architecture; similarly, context and heritage are underlined as key creative forces in design. The design practice seeks to re-establish the connection between people and their surroundings, and this is achieved through a meticulous treatment of light, material and, of course, space.

This is a concept sketch for The Sainsbury Laboratory, an 11,000 m^2 plant science research centre set in the Botanic Garden of the University of Cambridge. The simplicity and spontaneity of Stanton's preliminary draft belies the complex result. The design responds to its surroundings while also considering the multifarious scientific requirements of the building. It is intended to endorse an interaction between those working within the walls of the building and their landscape, a concept that is underscored by the open form that is developed within the sketch.

Concept Sketch: Sainsbury Laboratory Cambridge, 2007
Giclée print
20 × 50 cm

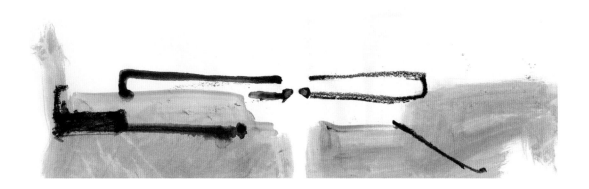

Frank Stella Hon RA

Born: 12 May 1936, Malden, Massachusetts, USA
Elected Honorary RA: 10 December 1993

Frank Stella was born in Massachusetts and studied at Princeton University, where he majored in History. After graduating in 1958 he moved to New York, where he absorbed the contemporary work on show in the city's art galleries, and in particular Jackson Pollock and Franz Kline. In 1970 he became the youngest ever artist to have a retrospective show in New York's Museum of Modern Art. He has gone on to have major survey shows across the USA, Europe and Japan, and in 2009 he was awarded the National Medal of Arts by the President of the United States, Barack Obama.

Stella is an artistic chameleon, continually reinventing himself over the course of his long career. He started out with an emphasis on the picture as an object, rather than as a representational vehicle. In the early 1960s he completed his *Black Painting* series, and declared that a picture was 'a flat surface with paint on it – nothing more'.

Although he has since shifted between phases of varying abstraction, this recent piece underlines his focus on the work of art being independent of both critical bolstering and representational specificity. The fine technique employed here of colour screenprint and stencil dates back to the mid-1960s, when Stella first started working with master printer Kenneth Tyler, and indeed his print work has done much to elevate the medium itself. This colourful image has a collage-like composition with layers and textures that play with the relationship between two and three dimensions that so fascinates Stella. The aesthetic exuberance of the piece feels consistent with his unwavering prioritisation of the intrinsic integrity of the work itself over any representative content, even if he now allows himself more than black paint and a blank canvas.

Stranz, 1999
107 colour screenprint and stencil (edition 13/28)
195.6 × 110.5 cm

Philip Sutton RA

Born: 20 October 1928, Poole, Dorset, UK
Elected ARA: 13 May 1977
Elected RA: 8 December 1988
Category of Membership: Painter

Philip Sutton studied at the Slade School of Fine Art, London. He travelled to Spain, France and Italy on scholarships before returning to teach at the school. His first solo show was held at Roland, Browse and Delbanco in 1956, the year he was elected a Member of the London Group. This was followed by many solo exhibitions throughout the UK including the Geffrye Museum, London (1959), a retrospective at Leeds City Art Gallery (1960), the Graves Art Gallery, Sheffield (1971) and more recently at the Richmond Hill Gallery, London (2007, 2009, 2010).

Sutton's commissions include the design for two tapestries at West Dean College, a London Transport Soho poster, a set of stamps for the Post Office, and a wall of tiles at the Art Tile Factory, Stoke-on-Trent. His work is held in collections around Britain including Birmingham City Art Gallery, Manchester City Art Gallery and Tate.

Travel has had a great influence on Sutton's work. In 1963 he moved with his family to Fiji. Although he only lived there for eleven months, it inspired the bright palette for which he is best known. For him it is the tool not only of representation, but of invention and imagination. Often translating landscapes, trees, and still-life into vibrant fantasies, Sutton's liberated attitude to colour recalls the work of the Fauves, and in particular Matisse. Sutton has said that the freedom to choose from a kaleidoscopic range of colour options makes him 'feel like a wild musician running through an orchestra, playing any instrument I wish'. Fond memories of Fiji as well as the delight that Sutton finds in painting is particularly manifest in this joyful coloured drawing of birds and trees in a garden in Manorbier in Pembrokeshire, where he now lives.

Fiji Comes to Manorbier, 1999
Ink and coloured pencil
30.5 × 40.8 cm

Fiji
Comes to
Pembrokeshire!

26·5·1999 –
Philip Snow

" THE GARDEN
MANORBIER "

Joe Tilson RA

Born: 24 August 1928, London, UK
Elected ARA: 20 May 1985
Elected RA: 26 June 1991
Category of Membership: Printmaker

Joe Tilson is a painter, sculptor and printmaker. He trained as a carpenter before completing National Service in the RAF. He then went on to study at St Martin's School of Art and the Royal College of Art, London, where he received the Rome Prize. He taught at St Martin's School of Art (1958–63) and subsequently at the Slade School of Fine Art, UCL and The School of Visual Arts, New York. His work is held in many international collections including Tate, The Museum of Modern Art, New York, and the Stedelijk, Amsterdam. He had a retrospective at the Royal Academy of Arts in 2002.

Tilson was one of the founding figures of British Pop Art. His work reflected the optimism and political activism that was characteristic of the 1960s. While embracing advances in technology and attitudes towards sexual liberation, he frustrated his tutors by refusing to be pinned down as a sculptor or a painter. A move to Italy in the 1970s changed his

work significantly, when he placed a new emphasis on the five elements and Greek and Roman mythology. However, his aim 'to make things that corresponded to my feelings and thoughts – not to pre-established categories' has remained consistent, and today he continues to work using grids as a structural device and with bold colours, emblematic imagery and the written word. Italy has also continued to have a significant influence on his formal vocabulary: 'Life [in Tuscany] is very vivid, things leap at you.'

In this particular piece the elements echo his iconic work *Zikkurat* from the late 1960s, while the wooden frame, left bare except for stencilled red numbers, is reminiscent of his 1970s' painting *Demetrius' Ladder*. Typical of Tilson's enduring style, each component has a structural, formal function as well as a symbolic meaning. The end product is visually harmonious and immediately appealing.

Finestra Veneziana San Sebastiano, 2007
Acrylic, Lattimo glass and Pietra d'Istria on wood relief
113 × 27.9 cm

David Tindle RA

Born: 29 April 1932, Huddersfield, Yorkshire, UK
Elected ARA: 27 April 1973
Elected RA: 9 May 1979
Category of Membership: Painter

David Tindle studied at Coventry School of Art, and later became a teacher in London at Hornsey College of Art and Byam Shaw School of Art. He was a visiting tutor at the Royal College of Art (1972–83) and Ruskin Master of Drawing at Oxford University (1985–87).

Tindle has had numerous solo exhibitions across the UK and Europe, his first at the Piccadilly Gallery in London in 1954. He has been part of key group shows including '25 Years of British Painting' at the Royal Academy of Arts in 1977 and 'New Acquisitions' at the National Portrait Gallery, London, in 1987.

Tindle has always shown sensitivity towards his canvas and his medium. Mostly working in egg tempera, he has developed a meticulous technique that results in subtle and delicate paintings, reflecting his attention to detail. He paints everyday scenes – still-lifes, landscapes and portraits – and most often the paintings possess a deeper level of meaning and verge on the surreal.

This painting is a multiple self-portrait. The muted colours do not overpower the subject-matter, the mood is quiet, understated and reflective. Despite this, the man's piercing stare emphasises the artist's scrutiny of age and the passing of time.

Portrait of a Man Looking, 2003
Egg tempera on cotton laid on panel
32.5 × 40.5 cm

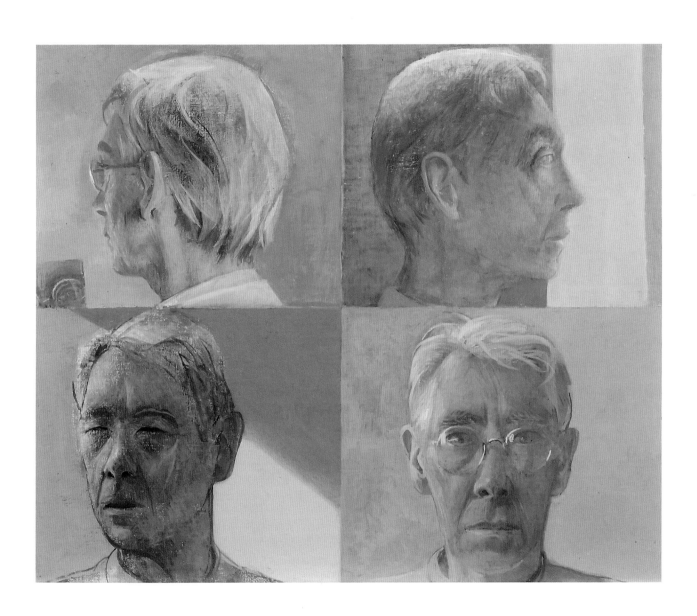

William Tucker RA

Born: 28 February 1935, Cairo, Egypt
Elected RA: 27 May 1992
Category of Membership: Sculptor

William Tucker gained a degree in History from Oxford before studying sculpture at St Martin's School of Art. Here he became associated with other young artists, such as Phillip King, Anthony Caro and David Annesley, who were trying to do something new with a medium that, at the time, was dominated by the figurative bronze tradition. Their ground-breaking predominantly abstract work, constructed from modern industrial materials and colourful, was first shown together at the Whitechapel Gallery in 1965 in the highly influential exhibition 'New Generation'. Tucker went on to have shows across Europe and the USA, representing Britain in the Venice Biennale of 1972. Collected by important public and private institutions worldwide, his contribution to sculpture has been recognised in several awards, most recently the New York Studio School (1999), the RA Summer Exhibition Sculpture Prize (2009), and the International Sculpture Center Lifetime Achievement Award (2010).

Tucker has also written and lectured extensively on sculpture. In 1975 he curated the 'The Condition of Sculpture' at the Hayward Gallery, where he championed the idea that sculpture should be an object – that is, something visually substantial that would actively seek to 'meet, attract and hold our sight'. This view held forth against the predominant conceptualism of the time. Later that decade Tucker moved to the United States, and since then his work has become larger, more monumental and increasingly sensual. His modelled forms cast in bronze hover between being abstract and figurative, with the reading changing depending on the viewer's position and understanding of the title.

Tucker is also a distinguished draughtsman. This fluid charcoal study is so evocative that we can almost feel the uncompromising solidity and undulating surface of one his bronze sculptures, as well as sense the brutal spirit of a bullfight.

Study for 'Tauromachy', 2007
Charcoal on paper
81 × 101.5 cm

Gillian Wearing RA

Born: 10 December 1963, Birmingham, UK
Elected RA: 11 December 2007
Category of Membership: Painter

In the trajectory of Gillian Wearing's celebrated career 1997 was a crucial year: she exhibited in the seminal 'Sensation' exhibition at the Royal Academy of Arts and won the Turner Prize.

An alumnus of Chelsea College of Art and Goldsmiths College, Wearing has carved out a reputation for witty personal revelation and intimate documentation of individual lives. Her first major work in 1992/3, *Signs that say what you want them to say and not Signs that say what someone else wants you to say*, involved stopping a random assortment of people in the street and encouraging them to compose signs expressing frank sentiments and emotions; Wearing then photographed the 'participants' with their signs. The much-celebrated, and pastiched, result set the tone for a body of work that is consistently entertaining and approachable.

This self-portrait is characteristic of Wearing's playful use of photography, while the array of poses reflects her recurrent exploration of the many sides of an individual, private and public, conscious and unconscious. There are also references to other works within Wearing's oeuvre, in particular her 1995 video piece *Homage to the woman with the bandaged face who I saw yesterday down Walworth Road* – a reportage performance piece in which she re-enacts a momentary interaction with a woman seen from the passenger seat of a car. The connection between the two works reminds us that, for Wearing, not only self-portraiture but all art is a self-conscious and self-reflexive exercise.

Self-portraits as Woman with Bandaged Face, 1995–2012
C-type print
39 × 106.8 cm

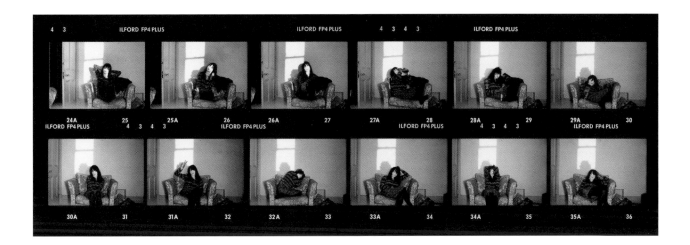

Anthony Whishaw RA

Born: 22 May 1930, London, UK
Elected ARA: 22 May 1980
Elected RA: 7 December 1989
Category of Membership: Painter

Anthony Whishaw studied at Chelsea School of Art and the Royal College of Art, London. During these years he received many awards, including a Royal College of Art Travelling Scholarship and Drawing Prize, Abbey Minor and Spanish Government Scholarships. He went on to have numerous solo and group exhibitions throughout the UK and beyond, most notably at Kettle's Yard, Cambridge, Galerie in Faust, Shanghai, China, and in London at the Barbican, the Whitechapel Gallery and the Hayward Gallery. His work is in collections across the world including Tate, National Gallery of Victoria, Melbourne Australia and the Government Art Collection.

Whishaw has always believed in the importance of experimentation and play in the search for unexpected visual ideas. A crucial turning-point occurred in the late 1960s when he changed medium from oil to acrylic and battled with the orthodoxy of American Abstract Expressionism, which demanded that painting should deny figuration while also enjoying the new freedom of Abstraction and Cubism.

Using illusion and allusion, past and present, spatial differences and multiple horizons he paints images ranging from 'nature and its forces to the attempted depiction of the moment before perception'.

'This painting', he says, 'is part of a group that radically changed the direction and intentions of my work, reintroducing extremes of tonal contrast, and visual ideas relating to the human presence, land/seascapes, trees and forces of nature. *Table Top with Dice* plays with light and disruptive space with the first appearance of tiny dots, pinpricks of light reflected from raindrops, leaves, flowers, stars etc., which are also used to lead the eye and peripheral vision around the work.'

Table Top with Dice, 1983–95
Acrylic, collage, oil on canvas
137 × 153 cm

Alison Wilding RA

Born: 7 July 1948, Blackburn, Lancashire, UK
Elected RA: 15 November 1999
Category of Membership: Sculptor

Alison Wilding trained at Nottingham College of Art, Ravensbourne College of Art and the Royal College of Art, where she specialised in sculpture. She has since exhibited extensively throughout the world in solo and group shows. Her first major solo exhibition was held at the Serpentine Gallery, London (1985), her first international solo show was at The Museum of Modern Art, New York (1987) and her first retrospective was at Tate, Liverpool (1991). She was shortlisted twice for the Turner Prize (1988 and 1992), and in 1998 she received a Henry Moore Fellowship for The British School at Rome.

Wilding started working on the *monocoque* series of sculptures (from the Greek for single – *mono*, and French for shell – *coque*) in 1990 initially to rid the work of its outer skin or surface in order to explore its interior. Materials range from cardboard to polished stainless steel and most recently laminated wood.

Monocoque is a construction technique that supports structural load by using an object's external skin (as opposed to using an internal frame or truss) that is then covered with a non-loadbearing skin. Most of the works are over life-sized and fabricated outside the studio, but the modest scale of *Rust* allowed Wilding to build the sculpture directly from a huge pile of laser-cut strips.

'In the air, the B-2 Stealth Bomber wears "a cloak of invisibility". Grounded, it is interpreted in *Rust* as much as a location, even an archaeological site, as a plane. Caught in the tight grid of its metal strips like a fly in a spider's web, is a scale model of the F117 Nighthawk fighter jet. I am drawn to the precision and performance of this abhorrent weaponry.'

Rust, 2008
Mild steel, plastic scale model
6.75 × 58 × 68 cm

Chris Wilkinson RA

Born: 1 July 1945, Amersham, Buckinghamshire, UK
Elected RA: 27 March 2006
Category of Membership: Architect

Chris Wilkinson is founding principal of Wilkinson Eyre Architects, a leading international architectural practice that has won over 150 design awards, including the prestigious RIBA Stirling Prize in two consecutive years – for the Magna Science Adventure Centre in 2001 and the Gateshead Millennium Bridge in 2002.

In London the practice has recently completed the Basketball Arena for the 2012 Olympic Games, Emirates Air Line Cable Car and The Crystal in the Royal Victoria Docks. Notable international buildings include the recently opened Singapore Gardens By the Bay and the Guangzhou IFC, which is the world's ninth tallest building.

Wilkinson was awarded an OBE in the Millennium Honours for services to architecture, made an Honorary Doctor of Westminster University in 2001, Doctor of Design at Oxford Brookes University in 2007 and Honorary Fellow of the American Institute of Architecture in 2007.

From Landscape to Portrait is a large-scale installation that prominently occupied the Royal Academy's Annenberg Courtyard for the 2012 'Summer Exhibition'. The concept is based on a narrative related to artists' frames, which rotate from landscape (horizontal format) to portrait (vertical format). Its sequential rotating geometry is intended to express movement, which is accentuated by its sinuous, reflective base structure.

From Landscape to Portrait, 2012
Model, constructed in acid-etched stainless steel
27.5 × 30 × 30 cm
Original watercolour sketch on paper
50 × 70 cm

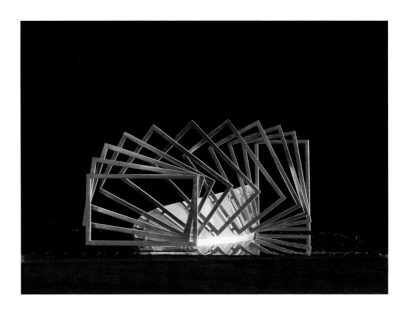

'FROM LANDSCAPE TO PORTRAIT'   CW 2012

Richard Wilson RA

Born: 24 May 1953, London, UK
Elected RA: 27 March 2006
Category of Membership: Sculptor

Richard Wilson is internationally celebrated for his interventions in architectural space that draw the large part of their inspiration from the worlds of engineering and construction. He has exhibited widely nationally and internationally, and represented Britain in the Sydney, São Paulo and Venice biennales, and Yokohama Triennale. He has twice been nominated for the Turner Prize, in 1988 and 1989. He was one of a select number of artists invited to create a major public work for the Millennium Dome, and the only British artist invited to participate in the Echigo-Tsumari Art Triennial (2000).

'What I actually do,' Wilson says, 'is tweak or undo or change the interiors of space (predominantly the interiors of museums and galleries when given permission) and in many instances actually enlist parts of the building as part of the sculpture, and in that way unsettle or break people's preconceptions of space, what they think space might be.'

In 2008 he created *Turning the Place Over* for Liverpool's Capital of Culture Year, for which this maquette was made. The sculpture consisted of a ten-metre-diameter ovoid cut from the façade of a building due to be demolished, and made to oscillate in three dimensions, offering recurrent glimpses of the interior during its constant cycle. As it rotated, the façade not only became completely inverted but moved into the building and out into the street, which was a disorientating and thrilling experience for those below as the building seemed to move towards and away from them.

Turning the Place Over. Maquette, 2007
Wood, metal, plastic and paint
59 × 59 × 40 cm

Bill Woodrow RA

Born: 1 November 1948, near Henley, Oxfordshire, UK
Elected RA: 28 May 2002
Category of Membership: Sculptor

Bill Woodrow studied at Winchester School of Art and at St Martin's School of Art, London, before spending one year at Chelsea School of Art. His first solo exhibition was at the Whitechapel Gallery and he has since shown work in prestigious galleries worldwide, including Tate Modern, Tate Britain, The Museum of Modern Art, New York, and the Martin-Gropius-Bau, Berlin. In the early 1980s he represented Britain at biennales in Sydney, Paris and São Paolo, and in 1986 he was a Turner Prize finalist.

Woodrow's sculptures are often characterised by his use of domestic and urban objects, where he leaves their original identities evident as well as the mode of their transformation. The juxtapositions of images and objects from ordinary life do not constitute didactic statements, but have an elliptical, poetic content. As Jon Wood writes: 'They are sculptures that operate as similes, made to be like things and sometimes mistaken for things. Woodrow works with similes, which gives sculptural stories a literalism that can be unsettling.'

There is certainly something unsettling about *Delphinium Evaluator*. In this bronze sculpture, both painted and patinated, a cow-like skull sits at the end of a delicate skeletal body formed by twigs and ridged with playing cards that seem to resemble vertebrae. The form rests on an unnatural bed of purple MDF, the colour of the poisonous delphinium plant – a regular cause of cattle deaths in the western United States. The simile is created and so too is the sense of unease. Woodrow states that he enjoys being 'literal, but to keep the thing sculptural at the same time… if this literalness creates a wobbly kind of feeling somewhere, I am not against that.'

Delphinium Evaluator, 2005
Bronze, laminated MDF, paint, shellac
46 × 117.6 × 100 cm

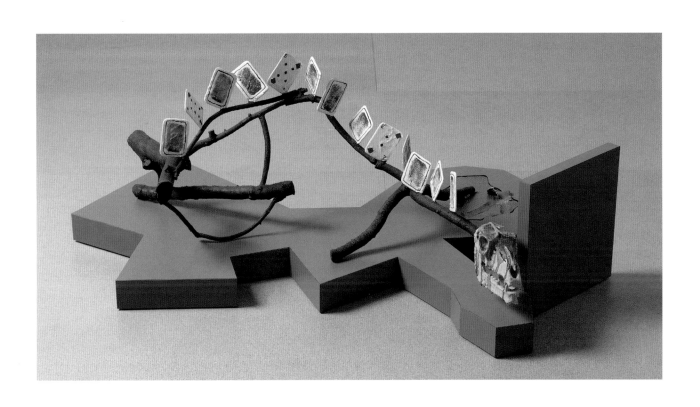

John Wragg RA

Born: 20 October 1937, York, UK
Elected ARA: 18 May 1983
Elected RA: 26 June 1991
Category of Membership: Sculptor

John Wragg studied at York School of Art and the Royal College of Art, London. He went on to win a number of prizes including a Sainsbury Award, and enjoyed successful shows at the Hanover Gallery, London, throughout the 1960s. His work encompasses both painting and sculpture and has been included in several significant international group shows. He is represented in numerous public collections including Israel Museum, Jerusalem, Tate, Wellington Art Gallery, New Zealand and the National Gallery of Modern Art, Edinburgh. He lives and works in Wiltshire.

Exploration and discovery is central to Wragg's art; he endeavours to express his 'endless preoccupation with the frailness and vulnerability of the human condition'. This is evident in his mediation between painting and sculpture, as well as his constant evaluation of the balance between figuration and abstraction. Wragg says: 'If the balance goes too far towards the abstract, there is the danger of it becoming a pretty object, making the tension ebb away.'

Blue Chair maintains its tension. We are lured towards a narrative, but ultimately kept at a distance. The isolated figure sits and stares defiantly back at the viewer, as if she is watching herself being painted. She is dressed as if she is about to go out; perhaps she is reluctant to wait for her image to be committed to canvas. The room, however, is anonymous – the walls and floor divide up the pictorial plane rather than describe detail. Although the same restless, elegant female appears in many of Wragg's recent paintings, formal and figurative devices shroud her in mystery.

Blue Chair, 2010
Acrylic on board
150 × 104 cm

Index

Royal Academy of Arts in London, 2012

Royal Academy of Arts

The Royal Academy of Arts has a unique position as an independent institution led by eminent artists and architects whose purpose is to promote the creation, enjoyment and appreciation of the visual arts through exhibitions, education and debate. The Royal Academy receives no annual funding via government, and is entirely reliant on self-generated income and charitable support.

You and/or your company can support the Royal Academy of Arts in a number of different ways:

- Almost £60 million has been raised for capital projects, including the Jill and Arthur M Sackler Wing, the restoration of the Main Galleries, the restoration of the John Madejski Fine Rooms, and the provision of better facilities for the display and enjoyment of the Academy's own collections of important works of art and documents charting the history of British art.
- Donations from individuals, trusts, companies and foundations also help support the Academy's internationally renowned exhibition programme, the conservation of the Collections and education projects for schools, families and people with special needs; as well as providing scholarships and bursaries for postgraduate art students in the Royal Academy Schools.
- As a company, you can invest in the Royal Academy through arts sponsorship, corporate membership and corporate entertaining, with specific opportunities that relate to your budgets and marketing or entertaining objectives.

- If you would like to preserve the Academy for future generations, please consider remembering us in your will. Your gift can be a sum of money, a specific item or a share of what is left after you have provided for your family and friends. Any gift, large or small, could help ensure that our work continues in the future.

To find out ways in which individuals can support this work, or a specific aspect of it, please contact Charlotte Appleyard, Head of Patrons, on 020 7300 5977.

To explore ways in which companies, trusts and foundations can become involved in the work of the Academy, please contact the Project Giving Office on 020 7300 5629/5979.

For more information on remembering the Academy in your will, please contact Emma Warren-Thomas on 020 7300 5677 or legacies@royalacademy.org.uk

Membership of the Friends

The Friends of the Royal Academy was founded in 1977 to support and promote the work of the Royal Academy. It is now one of the largest such organisations in the world, with around 90,000 members.

As a Friend you enjoy free entry to every RA exhibition and much more...

- Invites to Preview Days before exhibitions open to the public
- Bring one adult family guest and up to four family children under 16 to any exhibition for free
- Use of the Friends Room

- Receive the quarterly *RA Magazine*
- Access to a programme of Friends events
- Keep up to date with the Friends e-news, packed with events, news and offers

Why not join today?

- At the Friends desk in the Front Hall
- Online at www.royalacademy.org.uk/friends

- Ring 020 7300 5664 any day of the week
- E-mail friends.enquiries@royalacademy.org.uk

Credits

Co-ordinator
Allen Jones RA

Exhibition department
Edith Devaney (Curator)
Lorna Burn (Exhibition Manager)

Development
Sarah Cranmer
Michael Eldred
Sarah Grant Duff
Angharad Lloyd-Jones
Jane Marriott
Andrew McGowan

Communication
Will Dallimore

Catalogue entries
Lucy Archibald
Julien Domercq
Isabelle Kallo
Lily Le Brun
Alice Rowell
Robin Stewart
Emily Tobin

Editor
Abbie Coppard

Book design
01.02

Cover
Pentagram

Project management
Lisa Cherry
Bryony Harris
Rebecca King Lassman

Supported by
JTI

**Auction and
Catalogue Partner**
Sotheby's

With thanks to Anya Hindmarch

Burlington Benefactors
GAM (U.K.) LIMITED
John Pattisson
Philip and Val Marsden

Reynolds Benefactors
Ms Miel de Botton
The Lady Annie Colette Renwick
Virginia and David Slaymaker

Printed by
Henry Ling Limited, Dorchester

All information correct at
time of going to print

Photographic acknowledgements
Page 18, 40, 52, 54, 128, 186, 208, 212, 248: © Anne Purkiss
Page 19, 23, 27, 37, 47, 51, 63, 65, 69, 81, 85, 93, 95, 99, 101, 107, 111, 117, 135, 143, 155, 157, 161, 181, 183, 191, 195, 199, 207, 217, 239, 249: Photography Roy Fox & Alex Fox
Page 20: Portrait of Marina Abramović. © Marco Aneli, photographer. Courtesy the artist and Lisson Gallery
Page 21: © Marina Abramović. Courtesy Marina Abramović Archives and Lisson Gallery
Page 22, 24, 34, 38, 42, 44, 46, 48, 56, 58, 62, 64, 66, 76, 78, 80, 82, 86, 102, 106, 108, 110, 114, 118, 120, 122, 130, 132, 134, 136, 140, 146, 148, 154, 156, 160, 162, 164, 168, 170, 172, 174, 176, 178, 180, 184, 188, 192, 194, 196, 198, 204, 206, 210, 214, 218, 220, 226, 238, 240, 246, 252, 254, 256, 258: © Royal Academy of Arts, London. Photographer James Hunkin
Page 26, 84, 98, 104: © Royal Academy of Arts, London. Photographer Rob Petherick
Page 28, 50: © Martin Charles
Page 29: © Gillian Ayres. Courtesy Alan Cristea Gallery, London
Page 30: Photographer Thierry Bal
Page 31: Courtesy the artist and Hauser & Wirth
Page 32: Photographer Hugh Gilbert
Page 33: Photographer Peter Abrahams
Page 34: © John Bellany. Photographer Paul Bellany
Page 36, 68, 116: © Ander McIntyre
Page 39: Courtesy Ben Brown Fine Art, London
Page 41: Photographer Sally Jubb
Page 43: Photographer Michael Chevis
Page 53: © Barford Sculptures Ltd
Page 55: © The artist. Photographer John Riddy
Page 59: © David Chipperfield Architects
Page 60: © Royal Academy of Arts, London. Photographer Andrew Whittuck
Page 61: Photographer Peter Chinn
Page 70, 88, 124, 228: © Julian Anderson
Page 71: Courtesy the artist and Art First Gallery
Page 72: Photographer Richard Waite
Page 73, 259: Courtesy the artist
Page 74: © Red Saunders

Page 75: © Tony Cragg. Photographer Michael Richter
Page 77: © 2012 Michael Craig-Martin. Courtesy Gagosian Gallery
Page 83: Photographer John Bodkin
Page 87: Courtesy the artist and the Lisson Gallery
Page 89: Courtesy the artist and Frith Street Gallery, London. Photography Roy Fox & Alex Fox
Page 90, 144, 234: © Royal Academy of Arts, London. Photographer Marcus Leith
Page 91: Courtesy the artist, photographer Joss Bany
Page 92, 100: © Dennis Toff
Page 94: Courtesy John Donat/ RIBA Library Photographs Collection
Page 96: Kenneth Draper at Red Rocks, Menorca
Page 103: © The artist, courtesy White Cube. Photographer Ben Westoby
Page 109: Foster + Partners
Page 112: Courtesy dbox and Melissa Majchrzak Photography
Page 113: Image provided by Gehry Partners, LLP
Page 115: Photograph by Stephen White, London. © The artist
Page 119: © Anthony Green, c/o Whitcombe Associates
Page 125: © Photographer Hélène Binet
Page 126: Courtesy Cass Sculpture Foundation
Page 129 : © David Hockney
Page 137: © Paul Huxley. Photography Roy Fox & Alex Fox
Page 138: Photographer Philipp Ebeling
Page 141: The artist, courtesy of Gimpel Fils
Page 142: © Abe Frajndlich
Page 145: Photographer Sam Roberts
Page 149: © Allen Jones: *Enchanteresse* 2007
Page 150: © Nicholas Sinclair. All rights reserved, DACS, 2012
Page 151: Photographer Dave Morgan, courtesy of Anish Kapoor
Page 152: Photographer Renate Graf, courtesy White Cube. © Anselm Kiefer
Page 153: © The artist. Todd-White Art Photography, courtesy White Cube
Page 158, 159: © Jeff Koons
Page 166: Photographer Gautier Deblonde
Page 167: © The artist 2012
Page 169: © The artist
Page 175: © John Maine
Page 182: Photographer George McFadyen
Page 187: © The artist. Photography Roy Fox & Alex Fox
Page 193: Courtesy Galerie Lelong/ Photographer Fabrice Gibert
Page 200: Photographer Salvatore Licitra
Page 203: Courtesy the artist and Frith Street Gallery, London
Page 209: Courtesy the artist and Victoria Miro Gallery

Page 211: © Tom Phillips 2010. Photography Roy Fox & Alex Fox
Page 215: © Fiona Rae. Courtesy of Timothy Taylor Gallery, London
Page 216: Photographer Dudley Reed
Page 222, 223: Photographer Keith Rigley
Page 224: Courtesy the artist and Gagosian Gallery. Photographer Kate Simon
Page 225: © Ed Ruscha. Courtesy of the artist and Gagosian Gallery. Photographer Robert McKeever
Page 227: Courtesy Michael Sandle
Page 229: Image courtesy Gagosian Gallery. Photographer Mike Bruce. © 2012 Jenny Saville
Page 230: Terry Setch in his studio with recent painting *Tide Shift*, March 2012. Photography © David Knight
Page 231: Photography © Isabelle Anderson
Page 232: © Marc Seliger, 2005
Page 233: Courtesy the artist and Metro Pictures, NY
Page 236: © Kiriko Shirobayashi
Page 237: Photographer Adam Reich
Page 241: © Joe Tilson, courtesy Marlborough Fine Art
Page 242: Photographer Karin Szekessy
Page 244: Courtesy the artist and McKee Gallery, NY
Page 250: Alison Wilding and Stanley Jones at the Curwen Studio, Cambridge, (detail) © Andrew Lamb
Page 251: Photographer Pete White
Page 257: Courtesy the artist. Photographer Prudence Cuming Associates Ltd

Illustrations
Page 2: Tacita Dean, *Dead Budgie Project* (detail)
Page 4: Frank Stella, *Stranz* (detail)
Page 5: Chris Orr, *On the Road to Damascus, a London Fantasy based on Wenceslaus Hollar and Others* (detail)
Page 16-17: Humphrey Ocean, *Tangerine Static* (detail)

British Library
Cataloguing-in-publication Data
A catalogue record for this book is available in the British Library.

ISBN 978-1-907533-56-3